Agenta Millo

Python Programming For Artificial Intelligence

Practical Guides to Machine Learning Using AI

Table of Contents

Part 1: Foundations of Python for AI & Machine Learning

Chapter 1: Introduction to Python for AI

- Why Python for AI and Machine Learning?
- Understanding AI, Machine Learning, and Deep Learning
- Setting Up Your Python Environment
  - Anaconda, Jupyter Notebook, VS Code
- Installing Essential Libraries
  - NumPy, Pandas, Matplotlib
  - Scikit-Learn, TensorFlow, PyTorch

Chapter 2: Python Essentials for AI

- Data Types, Variables, and Operators
- Control Flow Statements (Loops, Conditionals, Functions)
- Object-Oriented Programming (OOP) for AI Development
- Working with Files and Data Formats
  - CSV, JSON, Pickle
- Error Handling and Debugging

Part 2: Data Science for Machine Learning

Chapter 3: Data Preprocessing & Cleaning

- Understanding Data: Structured vs. Unstructured
- Handling Missing Values, Duplicates, and Outliers
- Feature Scaling and Normalization
- Data Transformation Techniques
  - Encoding Categorical Variables, One-Hot Encoding
- Handling Large Datasets with Dask and Pandas

Chapter 4: Data Visualization for AI

- Introduction to Data Visualization Libraries
  - Matplotlib, Seaborn, Plotly
- Creating Charts and Graphs for Insights
- Correlation and Statistical Analysis
- Interactive Data Visualization for AI

Part 3: Supervised Learning: Training AI Models

Chapter 5: Introduction to Supervised Learning

- Training, Testing, and Validation
- Bias-Variance Tradeoff
- Overview of Key Supervised Learning Algorithms
- Steps in Building a Machine Learning Model

Chapter 6: Regression Models for AI

- Linear Regression and Polynomial Regression
- Ridge, Lasso, and Elastic Net Regression
- Evaluating Regression Models
  - MSE, RMSE, R^2 Score

Chapter 7: Classification Algorithms for AI

- Logistic Regression
- Decision Trees and Random Forest
- Support Vector Machines (SVM)
- Naïve Bayes and K-Nearest Neighbors (KNN)
- Model Evaluation Metrics
  - Confusion Matrix, Precision-Recall, F1 Score

Part 4: Unsupervised Learning: AI without Labels

Chapter 8: Clustering Techniques

- K-Means Clustering
- Hierarchical Clustering
- DBSCAN Algorithm

Chapter 9: Dimensionality Reduction

- Principal Component Analysis (PCA)
- t-Distributed Stochastic Neighbor Embedding (t-SNE)
- Autoencoders for Feature Reduction

Part 5: Deep Learning & Neural Networks

Chapter 10: Introduction to Deep Learning

- Neural Networks Basics
  - Perceptrons, Activation Functions
- Understanding Backpropagation and Gradient Descent

Chapter 11: Building Neural Networks with TensorFlow & PyTorch

- Setting Up Neural Networks with TensorFlow
- Training and Tuning Deep Learning Models
- PyTorch for Dynamic Neural Networks

Chapter 12: Convolutional Neural Networks (CNNs) for Image Recognition

- CNN Architecture
  - Convolution, Pooling, Fully Connected Layers
- Training a CNN for Image Classification

Chapter 13: Recurrent Neural Networks (RNNs) & Transformers for NLP

- Understanding Sequential Data & Time Series
- RNNs, LSTMs, and GRUs
- Introduction to Transformers
  - BERT, GPT

Part 6: AI Model Deployment & Real-World Applications

Chapter 14: AI Model Deployment

- Saving and Loading Models
  - Pickle, Joblib
- Deploying Models with Flask and FastAPI
- Model Monitoring & Performance Tuning

Chapter 15: Real-World AI Applications

- AI in Healthcare, Finance, and Business
- Ethical Considerations in AI

Chapter 1

Introduction to Python for AI

Why Python for AI and Machine Learning?

Artificial Intelligence (AI) and Machine Learning (ML) have become dominant forces in modern technology, driving innovation across industries like healthcare, finance, robotics, and automation. At the heart of this revolution lies **Python**, a versatile and powerful programming language widely recognized as the leading choice for AI and ML development.

1.1 Simplicity and Readability

Python's simple syntax and natural readability make it an excellent language for AI. Unlike languages such as C++ or Java, Python's code is concise, which allows developers to focus on solving AI-related problems rather than dealing with complex syntax. This readability accelerates development and reduces the learning curve, making it accessible to beginners and experts alike.

1.2 Comprehensive Libraries and Frameworks

One of Python's greatest strengths is its **rich ecosystem of AI and ML libraries**. These libraries eliminate the need to build models from scratch, enabling developers to use pre-built functions for data preprocessing, model training, and evaluation. Key libraries include:

- **NumPy** – Supports large, multi-dimensional arrays and provides mathematical functions.
- **Pandas** – Enables easy manipulation and analysis of structured data.
- **Matplotlib & Seaborn** – Provide data visualization capabilities.
- **Scikit-Learn** – A comprehensive ML library offering regression, classification, clustering, and more.
- **TensorFlow & PyTorch** – Leading deep learning frameworks for building neural networks.

1.3 Extensive Community Support

Python has a vast and active community of AI researchers, engineers, and contributors. This ensures that new AI techniques and improvements are quickly implemented into libraries. Additionally, platforms like Stack Overflow, GitHub, and specialized forums provide a wealth of resources for debugging and optimization.

1.4 Cross-Platform and Scalability

Python is cross-platform, meaning AI applications can be developed and deployed across various operating systems, including Windows, macOS, and Linux. It also supports cloud-based computing and parallel processing, allowing it to scale efficiently from small projects to enterprise-level AI solutions.

1.5 Integration with Other Technologies

Python seamlessly integrates with **big data technologies** (e.g., Hadoop, Apache Spark) and **cloud computing platforms** (e.g., AWS, Google Cloud, Azure), making it an ideal choice for large-scale AI applications.

Overview of AI, Machine Learning, and Deep Learning

Before diving into Python's implementation for AI, it's essential to understand the **fundamental concepts** of AI, ML, and Deep Learning. These terms are often used interchangeably but have distinct meanings.

2.1 What is Artificial Intelligence (AI)?

AI refers to **the simulation of human intelligence in machines**. It involves building algorithms that can perform tasks requiring human-like cognition, such as learning, reasoning, problem-solving, and decision-making. AI can be classified into three types:

1. **Narrow AI (Weak AI)** – Designed for specific tasks, such as chatbots, recommendation systems, and self-driving cars.
2. **General AI (Strong AI)** – Theoretical AI that can perform any intellectual task like a human.
3. **Super AI** – Hypothetical AI surpassing human intelligence, currently in the realm of science fiction.

2.2 What is Machine Learning (ML)?

Machine Learning is a **subset of AI** that enables computers to learn from data without explicit programming. Instead of following predefined rules, ML models recognize patterns in data and make predictions. ML is categorized into:

- **Supervised Learning** – Models learn from labeled datasets (e.g., spam detection, medical diagnoses).
- **Unsupervised Learning** – Models find patterns in unlabeled data (e.g., customer segmentation, anomaly detection).
- **Reinforcement Learning** – Models learn through rewards and punishments (e.g., robotics, game playing).

2.3 What is Deep Learning?

Deep Learning is a **subset of ML** that mimics the human brain's neural networks to process large datasets and recognize patterns. It is used in:

- **Computer Vision** – Image recognition, facial detection, autonomous vehicles.
- **Natural Language Processing (NLP)** – Chatbots, sentiment analysis, machine translation.
- **Speech Recognition** – Virtual assistants like Siri, Alexa, and Google Assistant.

Deep learning models typically require high computational power and large datasets, making frameworks like TensorFlow and PyTorch essential.

Setting Up Your Python Environment

To work on AI and ML projects efficiently, we need to set up a proper Python development environment. This involves **installing Python, choosing an Integrated Development Environment (IDE)**, and **configuring libraries**.

3.1 Installing Python

Most AI frameworks require **Python 3.x** (preferably the latest stable version). You can download Python from python.org.

Checking Python Installation

After installation, verify Python's version using:

```
bash
CopyEdit
python --version
```

or

```
bash
CopyEdit
python3 --version
```

3.2 Choosing an IDE

An **Integrated Development Environment (IDE)** is crucial for writing and running Python code efficiently. Recommended IDEs include:

Anaconda Distribution

- A powerful package that includes **Python, Jupyter Notebook, and essential libraries** for AI.
- Recommended for **beginners and data scientists**.

Jupyter Notebook

- A web-based interactive environment.
- Allows easy visualization of data and model outputs.
- Suitable for **data analysis and ML experiments**.

VS Code (Visual Studio Code)

- A lightweight, versatile editor with AI-specific extensions.
- Supports **debugging, Git integration, and cloud-based AI development**.

3.3 Installing Anaconda

Download and install **Anaconda** from anaconda.com. After installation, verify it with:

```
bash
CopyEdit
conda --version
```

To launch Jupyter Notebook, run:

bash
CopyEdit
```
jupyter notebook
```

Installing Essential Libraries

After setting up the environment, the next step is **installing necessary AI and ML libraries**.

4.1 Installing Libraries with pip

Use the following commands to install essential libraries:

bash
CopyEdit
```
pip install numpy pandas matplotlib seaborn scikit-learn
tensorflow torch
```

4.2 Key Libraries for AI and ML

Library	Purpose
NumPy	Numerical computing, array manipulations
Pandas	Data manipulation and analysis
Matplotlib & Seaborn	Data visualization
Scikit-Learn	Machine learning models and evaluation
TensorFlow	Deep learning and neural networks
PyTorch	Alternative deep learning framework

4.3 Verifying Library Installation

After installation, check if libraries are correctly installed by running the following in Python:

python
CopyEdit

```python
import numpy as np
import pandas as pd
import matplotlib.pyplot as plt
import tensorflow as tf
import torch

print("All libraries loaded successfully!")
```

If no errors occur, you are ready to begin working on AI and ML projects with Python.

Chapter 2

Python Essentials for AI

Python is the backbone of artificial intelligence and machine learning development. Before diving into AI-specific libraries and techniques, it is crucial to master Python's foundational elements. This chapter provides a comprehensive overview of **Python data types, control structures, object-oriented programming (OOP), file handling, and debugging techniques**, all of which are essential for building AI-driven applications.

Data Types, Variables, and Operators

2.1 Variables in Python

A variable in Python is a **named storage location** for data. Unlike statically-typed languages (such as Java or C++), Python dynamically assigns variable types based on the value assigned.

Declaring Variables
python
CopyEdit
```
x = 10        # Integer
y = 3.14      # Float
name = "AI"   # String
is_ready = True  # Boolean
```

Variables can change types during execution:

python
CopyEdit
```
x = 42        # Initially an integer
x = "Python"  # Now a string
```

Python's **dynamic typing** makes it flexible, but for large AI projects, using type hints improves code clarity:

python
CopyEdit
```python
def add(a: int, b: int) -> int:
    return a + b
```

2.2 Data Types in Python

Data Type	Example	Usage in AI
Integer (int)	x = 10	Storing counts, indexing
Float (float)	y = 3.14	Probabilities, statistical measures
String (str)	text = "AI"	Text processing in NLP
Boolean (bool)	flag = True	Decision-making, binary classification
List (list)	nums = [1,2,3]	Data storage, feature sets
Tuple (tuple)	coords = (3, 4)	Immutable data storage
Dictionary (dict)	data = {"name": "AI"}	Storing structured data
Set (set)	unique_vals = {1,2,3}	Eliminating duplicates

Lists and dictionaries are commonly used in **AI datasets and preprocessing tasks**.

Example: Using Lists and Dictionaries in AI
python
CopyEdit
```python
dataset = [
```

```
    {"id": 1, "label": "cat", "features": [0.1, 0.2, 0.3]},
    {"id": 2, "label": "dog", "features": [0.4, 0.5, 0.6]},
]
```

2.3 Operators in Python

Python provides **arithmetic, logical, comparison, bitwise, and assignment operators**, all of which are crucial in AI computations.

Arithmetic Operators
python
CopyEdit
```
a = 10
b = 3
print(a + b)   # Addition
print(a - b)   # Subtraction
print(a * b)   # Multiplication
print(a / b)   # Division
print(a ** b) # Exponentiation
```

Comparison and Logical Operators
python
CopyEdit
```
x = 5
y = 10

print(x > y)   # False
print(x < y and y > 8)   # True
print(not (x == y))   # True
```

These operators are often used in **decision-making and AI model evaluations**.

Control Flow Statements (Loops, Conditionals, Functions)

3.1 Conditional Statements

Conditionals allow AI models to make **decisions** based on conditions.

```python
CopyEdit
score = 85
if score > 90:
    print("Excellent")
elif score > 75:
    print("Good")
else:
    print("Needs Improvement")
```

AI models use conditionals in **classification, decision trees, and anomaly detection**.

3.2 Loops: For and While

Loops iterate over data structures, a common requirement in **data processing and training AI models**.

For Loop
```python
CopyEdit
for i in range(5):
    print(f"Iteration {i}")
```

While Loop
```python
CopyEdit
x = 5
while x > 0:
    print(f"Countdown: {x}")
    x -= 1
```

3.3 Functions in Python

Functions **modularize AI code**, improving maintainability.

python
CopyEdit
```python
def preprocess_data(data):
    return [x / 100 for x in data]  # Normalize features

features = [10, 20, 30]
print(preprocess_data(features))
```

Python also supports **lambda functions**, useful for quick computations:

python
CopyEdit
```python
square = lambda x: x ** 2
print(square(5))  # 25
```

Object-Oriented Programming (OOP) for AI Development

4.1 What is OOP?

Object-Oriented Programming (OOP) organizes AI models using **classes and objects**.

4.2 Creating a Class in Python

python
CopyEdit
```python
class NeuralNetwork:
    def __init__(self, layers):
        self.layers = layers

    def train(self, data):
        print(f"Training on {len(data)} samples")

nn = NeuralNetwork([3, 5, 2])
nn.train([1, 2, 3, 4])
```

OOP is crucial in **AI frameworks** like TensorFlow and PyTorch.

Working with Files and Data Formats (CSV, JSON, Pickle)

5.1 Reading and Writing CSV Files

CSV files store structured data, commonly used in **AI datasets**.

python
CopyEdit
```python
import pandas as pd

data = pd.read_csv("dataset.csv")
print(data.head())
```

5.2 Working with JSON Files

JSON is used for **storing AI model configurations**.

python
CopyEdit
```python
import json

config = {"learning_rate": 0.01, "epochs": 10}
with open("config.json", "w") as f:
    json.dump(config, f)
```

5.3 Using Pickle to Save AI Models

Pickle saves **trained AI models** for reuse.

python
CopyEdit
```python
import pickle

model = {"weights": [0.1, 0.2, 0.3]}
with open("model.pkl", "wb") as f:
    pickle.dump(model, f)
```

Error Handling and Debugging

6.1 Try-Except for Error Handling

AI applications must **handle errors** gracefully.

python
CopyEdit
```python
try:
    result = 10 / 0   # Division by zero error
except ZeroDivisionError as e:
    print(f"Error: {e}")
```

6.2 Debugging with Print and Logging

Using **print statements** or **logging** helps track AI errors.

python
CopyEdit
```python
import logging

logging.basicConfig(level=logging.INFO)
logging.info("Training started...")
```

6.3 Using Debugging Tools

Python's pdb module helps **step through AI code**.

```python
CopyEdit
import pdb

def divide(a, b):
    pdb.set_trace()  # Debugging breakpoint
    return a / b

divide(10, 2)
```

Summary of Key Concepts in Python for AI

Concept	Importance in AI
Data Types & Variables	Manage and store AI-related data
Control Flow Statements	Enable decision-making and iteration
Functions	Modularize AI preprocessing and training steps
OOP	Used in building AI models and frameworks
File Handling	Read and store AI datasets
Debugging	Improve reliability and efficiency of AI programs

This chapter builds the **Python foundation necessary for AI development**. In the next chapter, we will explore **data preprocessing and visualization**, essential steps before feeding data into machine learning models.

Chapter 3

Data Preprocessing & Cleaning

Data is the foundation of machine learning and artificial intelligence. The quality of data directly impacts the accuracy and reliability of AI models. Before training a machine learning model, raw data must be **cleaned, transformed, and structured** to ensure that it is useful for analysis. This chapter covers **understanding data types, handling missing values, dealing with duplicates and outliers, feature scaling, encoding categorical variables, and working with large datasets using Dask and Pandas.**

Understanding Data (Structured vs. Unstructured Data)

3.1 What is Data?

Data refers to any **collection of facts, statistics, or information** that can be processed by a computer. In the AI and machine learning world, data is the primary resource that helps models learn patterns and make predictions.

3.2 Types of Data

Structured Data

Structured data is **highly organized and stored in a predefined format**, typically in relational databases or spreadsheets. It follows a strict schema with clearly defined rows and columns.

- **Examples:**
  - Customer records in an Excel sheet
  - Sales transactions in a SQL database
  - Sensor readings from IoT devices
- **Example of Structured Data in Pandas:**

```python
CopyEdit
import pandas as pd
```

```python
data = pd.DataFrame({
    "Customer_ID": [101, 102, 103],
    "Name": ["Alice", "Bob", "Charlie"],
    "Purchase_Amount": [250.50, 340.75, 120.90]
})

print(data)
```

Unstructured Data

Unstructured data **does not follow a specific format** and is difficult to organize into tables. It requires advanced techniques like **Natural Language Processing (NLP)** and **Computer Vision (CV)** for meaningful insights.

- **Examples:**
  - Text data (emails, social media posts, articles)
  - Image and video data
  - Audio recordings
- **Example of Unstructured Data (Text Analysis in Python)**

python
CopyEdit
```python
text_data = ["This is an AI book.", "Machine Learning is
fascinating!", "Deep Learning is powerful."]
for text in text_data:
    print(f"Text Length: {len(text)}")
```

3.3 Semi-Structured Data

Semi-structured data contains elements of both structured and unstructured data. It has an **irregular structure but contains metadata** that can be processed easily.

- **Examples:**
  - JSON and XML files
  - Log files from web servers
  - NoSQL databases like MongoDB
- **Example of Semi-Structured Data (JSON in Python)**

```
python
CopyEdit
import json

data = {
    "user": "Alice",
    "transactions": [
        {"item": "Laptop", "amount": 1200},
        {"item": "Phone", "amount": 800}
    ]
}

print(json.dumps(data, indent=2))
```

Handling Missing Values, Duplicates, and Outliers

Real-world datasets are often incomplete, with missing values, duplicate records, or extreme values (outliers) that can negatively impact model performance.

4.1 Handling Missing Values

Missing data occurs when values are unavailable in a dataset. The three main approaches to handling missing values are:

1. **Removing Missing Values**

```
python
CopyEdit
df.dropna(inplace=True)   # Removes rows with missing values
```

2. **Filling Missing Values with Mean/Median**

```
python
CopyEdit
df['Age'].fillna(df['Age'].mean(), inplace=True)   # Replaces
missing values with column mean
```

17

3. **Using Interpolation for Time-Series Data**

python
CopyEdit
```
df.interpolate(method='linear', inplace=True)  # Fills missing
values using linear interpolation
```

4.2 Handling Duplicate Records

Duplicate records can distort model training and lead to **biased results**.

- **Detecting Duplicates**

python
CopyEdit
```
duplicates = df.duplicated()
print(df[duplicates])  # Shows duplicate rows
```

- **Removing Duplicates**

python
CopyEdit
```
df.drop_duplicates(inplace=True)
```

4.3 Handling Outliers

Outliers are extreme values that deviate significantly from other observations. They can **skew statistical analysis and predictions**.

Detecting Outliers Using the Interquartile Range (IQR)
python
CopyEdit
```
Q1 = df["Price"].quantile(0.25)
Q3 = df["Price"].quantile(0.75)
IQR = Q3 - Q1

# Define lower and upper bound
lower_bound = Q1 - 1.5 * IQR
upper_bound = Q3 + 1.5 * IQR
```
18

```
outliers = df[(df["Price"] < lower_bound) | (df["Price"] >
upper_bound)]
print(outliers)
```

- **Removing Outliers**

python
CopyEdit
```
df = df[(df["Price"] >= lower_bound) & (df["Price"] <=
upper_bound)]
```

Feature Scaling and Normalization

Feature scaling ensures that numerical features have the **same scale** to prevent biased learning in machine learning models.

5.1 Standardization (Z-Score Normalization)

Standardization transforms features to have a **mean of 0 and standard deviation of 1**.

python
CopyEdit
```
from sklearn.preprocessing import StandardScaler

scaler = StandardScaler()
df_scaled = scaler.fit_transform(df[["Age", "Salary"]])
```

5.2 Min-Max Normalization

Scales values between **0 and 1**, useful for algorithms like **neural networks**.

python
CopyEdit
```
from sklearn.preprocessing import MinMaxScaler
```

```
scaler = MinMaxScaler()
df_normalized = scaler.fit_transform(df[["Age", "Salary"]])
```

Data Transformation Techniques (Encoding Categorical Variables, One-Hot Encoding)

6.1 Label Encoding

Converts categorical labels into **numeric form**.

python
CopyEdit
```
from sklearn.preprocessing import LabelEncoder

encoder = LabelEncoder()
df["Category"] = encoder.fit_transform(df["Category"])
```

6.2 One-Hot Encoding

Creates **binary columns** for each category.

python
CopyEdit
```
df = pd.get_dummies(df, columns=["Category"], drop_first=True)
```

Handling Large Datasets with Dask and Pandas

When working with massive datasets, **Pandas** may struggle with memory limitations. **Dask** provides parallel processing to efficiently handle large data.

7.1 Using Dask for Large Datasets

python
CopyEdit
```
import dask.dataframe as dd
```

```
df = dd.read_csv("large_dataset.csv")
df.head()
```

7.2 Processing Large Dataframes with Dask

python
CopyEdit
```
df_grouped = df.groupby("Category").mean().compute()
print(df_grouped)
```

7.3 Comparing Pandas vs. Dask Performance

Feature	Pandas	Dask
Dataset Size	Small to Medium	Large to Very Large
Speed	Fast for small data	Optimized for large-scale data
Parallel Computing	No	Yes
Out-of-Memory Processing	No	Yes

Key Takeaways

Concept	Importance in AI
Structured vs. Unstructured Data	Defines data types for different AI models
Handling Missing Data	Prevents biased and inaccurate predictions
Dealing with Outliers	Reduces skewness in model performance
Feature Scaling	Ensures fair comparisons between features
Encoding Categorical Data	Converts text into numerical format for ML models
Dask for Large Data	Enables scalable data processing

By understanding data preprocessing techniques, we ensure **clean, structured, and optimized data** for AI and ML models. The next chapter will explore **data visualization techniques to gain insights before training models.**

Chapter 4

Data Visualization for AI

Data visualization plays a crucial role in Artificial Intelligence (AI) and Machine Learning (ML) by allowing data scientists and engineers to **explore datasets, detect patterns, and interpret model results effectively**. Without visualization, raw data remains difficult to analyze, and AI models become harder to interpret. This chapter covers **essential data visualization libraries, techniques for creating informative graphs, correlation analysis, and interactive visualization tools for AI applications.**

Introduction to Data Visualization Libraries (Matplotlib, Seaborn, Plotly)

Python offers several powerful libraries for **visualizing data** in AI projects. Some of the most widely used libraries include **Matplotlib, Seaborn, and Plotly**.

4.1 Matplotlib: The Foundation of Data Visualization

Matplotlib is the most fundamental plotting library in Python, providing a **low-level interface** for creating static, animated, and interactive visualizations.

Installing Matplotlib
bash
CopyEdit
```
pip install matplotlib
```

Basic Matplotlib Example
python
CopyEdit
```
import matplotlib.pyplot as plt

# Sample data
years = [2015, 2016, 2017, 2018, 2019, 2020]
sales = [100, 150, 200, 250, 300, 400]
```

23

```
# Create a line plot
plt.plot(years, sales, marker='o', linestyle='-', color='b',
label='Sales Growth')
plt.xlabel('Year')
plt.ylabel('Sales')
plt.title('Company Sales Over Time')
plt.legend()
plt.show()
```

Matplotlib is commonly used for **basic static charts**, such as **line plots, bar charts, histograms, and scatter plots**.

4.2 Seaborn: Statistical Data Visualization

Seaborn is built on top of Matplotlib and provides **advanced statistical visualization tools** with better aesthetics.

Installing Seaborn
bash
CopyEdit
```
pip install seaborn
```

Seaborn Example: Creating a Histogram
python
CopyEdit
```
import seaborn as sns
import pandas as pd

# Sample dataset
data = pd.DataFrame({
    'age': [22, 25, 47, 35, 29, 41, 50, 28, 34, 30]
})

# Create a histogram
sns.histplot(data['age'], bins=5, kde=True)
```
24

```
plt.title('Age Distribution')
plt.show()
```

Seaborn is ideal for **statistical plots like histograms, heatmaps, violin plots, and pair plots**.

4.3 Plotly: Interactive Visualization

Plotly is a **highly interactive** visualization library often used in **AI dashboards and web applications**.

Installing Plotly
bash
CopyEdit
```
pip install plotly
```

Plotly Example: Interactive Line Chart
python
CopyEdit
```
import plotly.express as px
import pandas as pd

# Sample data
df = pd.DataFrame({'Year': [2015, 2016, 2017, 2018, 2019, 2020],
                   'Sales': [100, 150, 200, 250, 300, 400]})

fig = px.line(df, x='Year', y='Sales', title="Sales Over Time",
markers=True)
fig.show()
```

Plotly is commonly used for **dynamic AI dashboards, web-based applications, and real-time AI analytics**.

Creating Charts and Graphs for Insights

AI and machine learning involve **analyzing large datasets**. Visualization techniques help in **identifying trends, relationships, and anomalies** in data.

5.1 Line Plots for Time Series Data

Line plots are useful for tracking **trends over time**.

python
CopyEdit
```
plt.plot(df["Year"], df["Sales"], marker='o', color='g')
plt.xlabel("Year")
plt.ylabel("Sales")
plt.title("Company Sales Over Years")
plt.show()
```

Use Cases in AI:

- Stock market price trends
- Weather predictions
- AI model performance over training epochs

5.2 Bar Charts for Categorical Data

Bar charts compare different categories, often used in **AI model evaluation and feature analysis**.

python
CopyEdit
```
categories = ['Dogs', 'Cats', 'Birds']
counts = [50, 75, 30]

plt.bar(categories, counts, color=['red', 'blue', 'green'])
plt.xlabel("Animal Type")
plt.ylabel("Count")
plt.title("Animal Adoption Rates")
plt.show()
```

Use Cases in AI:

- Feature importance visualization
- Sentiment analysis breakdown
- Model comparison

5.3 Histograms for Distribution Analysis

Histograms help analyze **data distribution**, useful in AI preprocessing.

python
CopyEdit
```python
sns.histplot(df["Sales"], bins=10, kde=True)
plt.title("Sales Distribution")
plt.show()
```

Use Cases in AI:

- Normalizing data distributions
- Identifying skewness in datasets
- Visualizing class imbalances

5.4 Scatter Plots for Relationship Analysis

Scatter plots show relationships between two numerical variables, helping AI practitioners understand **correlations**.

python
CopyEdit
```python
import numpy as np

# Sample data
x = np.random.rand(50)
y = 2*x + np.random.normal(0, 0.1, 50)
```

```
plt.scatter(x, y, color='blue', alpha=0.5)
plt.xlabel("Feature 1")
plt.ylabel("Feature 2")
plt.title("Scatter Plot of Feature Relationships")
plt.show()
```

Use Cases in AI:

- Finding correlations in datasets
- Visualizing decision boundaries in classification problems
- Detecting data clustering patterns

Correlation and Statistical Analysis

Correlation analysis measures the **relationship between variables**, crucial in AI for **feature selection and model performance tuning**.

6.1 Heatmaps for Correlation Analysis

Heatmaps display correlation between features in a dataset.

python
CopyEdit
```
import seaborn as sns
import numpy as np

# Sample correlation matrix
data = np.random.rand(10, 10)
sns.heatmap(data, annot=True, cmap="coolwarm")
plt.title("Feature Correlation Heatmap")
plt.show()
```

Use Cases in AI:

- Understanding feature importance
- Removing redundant or highly correlated features
- Improving model generalization

6.2 Pair Plots for Multivariate Analysis

Pair plots help visualize relationships between multiple variables.

python
CopyEdit
```
sns.pairplot(df)
plt.show()
```

Use Cases in AI:

- Exploring feature relationships
- Detecting non-linear dependencies
- Identifying outliers

Interactive Data Visualization for AI

7.1 Using Plotly for Interactive Dashboards

Interactive dashboards allow **real-time AI model monitoring**.

python
CopyEdit
```
import plotly.express as px

df = px.data.gapminder()
fig = px.scatter(df, x="gdpPercap", y="lifeExp",
color="continent", hover_name="country", log_x=True,
size_max=60)
fig.show()
```

Use Cases in AI:

- Real-time AI model monitoring
- Dynamic AI dashboards for insights
- Interactive feature selection

7.2 Using Streamlit for AI Model Visualization

Streamlit allows easy creation of AI model visualizations.

bash
CopyEdit
```bash
pip install streamlit
```

python
CopyEdit
```python
import streamlit as st

st.title("AI Model Performance Dashboard")
st.line_chart(df["Sales"])
```

Run the script:

bash
CopyEdit
```bash
streamlit run script.py
```

Key Takeaways from Data Visualization in AI

Visualization Type	Best Use Case
Line Plots	Time-series trends (model accuracy, stock prices)
Bar Charts	Categorical comparisons (feature importance, sentiment analysis)
Histograms	Distribution analysis (skewness, normalization)
Scatter Plots	Relationship analysis (correlation, decision boundaries)
Heatmaps	Feature correlation (multicollinearity analysis)
Interactive Dashboards	Real-time AI monitoring

With **proper visualization techniques**, AI practitioners can gain **deeper insights** into datasets, optimize feature selection, and enhance **model interpretability**. The next chapter will cover **Supervised Learning and AI Model Training Techniques**.

Chapter 5

Introduction to Supervised Learning

Supervised learning is one of the most fundamental paradigms in machine learning, where an algorithm learns patterns from labeled data to make future predictions. This chapter covers the **concept of training, testing, and validation**, explores the **bias-variance tradeoff**, provides an **overview of key supervised learning algorithms**, and outlines the **step-by-step process of building a machine learning model**. Understanding these principles is essential for designing accurate and robust AI models.

Understanding the Concept of Training, Testing, and Validation

5.1 What is Supervised Learning?

Supervised learning is a type of machine learning where an algorithm learns from **labeled training data**. The goal is to **map input features (X) to output labels (Y)** by identifying patterns in the data.

- **Input (X):** Features or independent variables (e.g., age, income, education level)
- **Output (Y):** Target variable or dependent variable (e.g., purchase decision, disease diagnosis)

Example of Supervised Learning:

- Predicting house prices based on **square footage, number of rooms, and location**.
- Classifying emails as **spam or not spam** based on their content.
- Diagnosing diseases based on **symptoms and medical records**.

Supervised learning can be divided into two main categories:

1. **Regression:** Predicts continuous values (e.g., predicting house prices).

2. **Classification:** Predicts discrete categories (e.g., classifying emails as spam or non-spam).

5.2 Training, Testing, and Validation

To develop a machine learning model, we split data into three key sets:

Dataset Type	Purpose	Typical Split
Training Set	Used to train the model	70-80% of the data
Validation Set	Used to tune hyperparameters and avoid overfitting	10-15% of the data
Test Set	Used to evaluate final model performance	10-15% of the data

Splitting Data in Python

python

CopyEdit

```
from sklearn.model_selection import train_test_split

import pandas as pd


# Load dataset

df = pd.read_csv("dataset.csv")
```

```
# Split features (X) and target (Y)

X = df.drop(columns=["target"])

y = df["target"]


# Perform train-test split (80% training, 20% testing)

X_train, X_test, y_train, y_test = train_test_split(X, y,
test_size=0.2, random_state=42)


print("Training Set Size:", X_train.shape)

print("Test Set Size:", X_test.shape)
```

Using a **validation set** is crucial when tuning hyperparameters, especially for deep learning models.

Bias-Variance Tradeoff

6.1 Understanding Bias and Variance

The **bias-variance tradeoff** is a fundamental concept in machine learning that balances model simplicity and complexity.

Term	Description	Effect on Model
Bias	Error from overly simplistic models (e.g., linear regression)	High bias → Underfitting
Varia nce	Error from overly complex models (e.g., deep neural networks)	High variance → Overfitting

A model with **high bias** fails to learn patterns (underfitting), while a model with **high variance** memorizes the training data but performs poorly on unseen data (overfitting).

6.2 Visualizing the Bias-Variance Tradeoff

A model's performance depends on finding a balance between bias and variance.

6.3 Managing Bias and Variance

- **To Reduce Bias (Underfitting):**
    - Use more complex models (e.g., decision trees, deep learning).
    - Provide more features or engineer better representations.
    - Train for more epochs (in deep learning).
- **To Reduce Variance (Overfitting):**
    - Use simpler models (e.g., linear regression instead of neural networks).
    - Increase training data.
    - Apply regularization techniques like **L1/L2 penalties** or **dropout**.

Example: Controlling Overfitting in a Decision Tree

python

```
from sklearn.tree import DecisionTreeClassifier

# Create a Decision Tree with depth limitation

model = DecisionTreeClassifier(max_depth=5)

model.fit(X_train, y_train)
```

Overview of Key Supervised Learning Algorithms

7.1 Regression Algorithms (Predicting Continuous Values)

Algorithm	Use Case
Linear Regression	Predicting house prices, stock market trends
Polynomial Regression	Modeling complex relationships between variables
Ridge/Lasso Regression	Handling multicollinearity in regression

Example: Linear Regression

python

CopyEdit

```
from sklearn.linear_model import LinearRegression

model = LinearRegression()

model.fit(X_train, y_train)
```

7.2 Classification Algorithms (Predicting Categories)

Algorithm	Use Case
Logistic Regression	Email spam detection, disease classification
Decision Trees	Customer segmentation, loan approval prediction
Random Forest	Fraud detection, recommender systems
Support Vector Machines (SVM)	Image classification, face recognition
Naïve Bayes	Text classification (spam detection, sentiment analysis)
K-Nearest Neighbors (KNN)	Handwriting recognition, recommendation systems

Example: Random Forest Classifier

python

```
from sklearn.ensemble import RandomForestClassifier

model = RandomForestClassifier(n_estimators=100)

model.fit(X_train, y_train)
```

Each algorithm has **strengths and weaknesses**, and choosing the right one depends on the dataset and problem complexity.

Steps in Building a Machine Learning Model

Step 1: Data Collection

Gather structured or unstructured data from sources like **databases, APIs, or web scraping**.

Step 2: Data Preprocessing

- Handle **missing values, duplicates, and outliers**.
- Apply **feature scaling and normalization** for numerical stability.
- Encode **categorical variables** into numerical format.

Example: Data Preprocessing in Python

python

CopyEdit

```
from sklearn.preprocessing import StandardScaler


scaler = StandardScaler()

X_train_scaled = scaler.fit_transform(X_train)
```

Step 3: Model Selection

Choose a suitable supervised learning algorithm based on the **problem type (regression or classification)**.

Step 4: Training the Model

Fit the model to the training data.

python

CopyEdit

```python
model.fit(X_train_scaled, y_train)
```

Step 5: Model Evaluation

Evaluate performance using metrics like **accuracy, precision, recall, RMSE**.

python

CopyEdit

```python
from sklearn.metrics import accuracy_score

y_pred = model.predict(X_test)

print("Accuracy:", accuracy_score(y_test, y_pred))
```

Step 6: Hyperparameter Tuning

Optimize model performance using techniques like **grid search, random search, or Bayesian optimization**.

python

CopyEdit

```python
from sklearn.model_selection import GridSearchCV


param_grid = {'n_estimators': [50, 100, 150]}
```

```
grid = GridSearchCV(RandomForestClassifier(), param_grid)

grid.fit(X_train, y_train)
```

Step 7: Model Deployment

Once optimized, the trained model is deployed in **real-world applications, APIs, or cloud platforms**.

python

CopyEdit

```
import pickle


# Save the trained model

with open('model.pkl', 'wb') as f:

    pickle.dump(model, f)
```

Key Takeaways from Supervised Learning

Concept	Importance
Train-Test Split	Prevents overfitting and ensures generalization
Bias-Variance Tradeoff	Balances model complexity and accuracy

Regression Algorithms	Predict continuous values
Classification Algorithms	Predict categorical outcomes
Hyperparameter Tuning	Optimizes model performance

By following these steps, AI practitioners can develop **robust supervised learning models** for real-world applications. The next chapter will explore **specific regression models for AI and their applications**.

Chapter 6

Regression Models for AI

Regression models form the foundation of many artificial intelligence (AI) applications where the goal is to predict continuous values. From predicting **house prices** and **stock market trends** to **estimating patient survival rates**, regression techniques are widely used in machine learning. This chapter will explore **linear regression, polynomial regression, Ridge, Lasso, and Elastic Net regression**, along with essential techniques for evaluating regression models using **Mean Squared Error (MSE), Root Mean Squared Error (RMSE), and R² Score**.

Linear Regression and Polynomial Regression

6.1 Linear Regression

Linear regression is the most fundamental regression algorithm that models the relationship between **independent variables (features)** and **dependent variables (targets)** using a straight-line equation:

$$Y = b_0 + b_1 X_1 + b_2 X_2 + \cdots + b_n X_n$$

where:

- YYY is the predicted value (target variable).
- X1,X2,...,XnX_1, X_2, ..., X_nX1,X2,...,Xn are input features.
- b0b_0b0 (intercept) and b1,b2,...,bnb_1, b_2, ..., b_nb1,b2,...,bn (coefficients) are model parameters.

Example: Simple Linear Regression

Predicting house prices based on square footage:

python
CopyEdit
```
import numpy as np
```
42

```python
import pandas as pd
import matplotlib.pyplot as plt
from sklearn.linear_model import LinearRegression
from sklearn.model_selection import train_test_split

# Sample dataset
data = {'Square_Feet': [800, 1000, 1200, 1500, 1800, 2000],
        'Price': [150000, 180000, 210000, 250000, 290000,
320000]}

df = pd.DataFrame(data)

# Splitting data
X = df[['Square_Feet']]
y = df['Price']
X_train, X_test, y_train, y_test = train_test_split(X, y,
test_size=0.2, random_state=42)

# Training model
model = LinearRegression()
model.fit(X_train, y_train)

# Predictions
y_pred = model.predict(X_test)

# Plotting regression line
plt.scatter(df['Square_Feet'], df['Price'], color='blue',
label="Actual Prices")
plt.plot(X_test, y_pred, color='red', linewidth=2,
label="Regression Line")
plt.xlabel("Square Feet")
plt.ylabel("Price")
plt.legend()
plt.show()
```

6.2 Polynomial Regression

Linear regression is limited to **linear relationships** between variables. However, many real-world scenarios involve **non-linear relationships**. Polynomial regression extends linear regression by introducing higher-order terms:

$$Y = b_0 + b_1 X + b_2 X^2 + b_3 X^3 + \cdots + b_n X^n$$

where **higher-degree polynomials** allow the model to fit curved data.

Example: Polynomial Regression
python
CopyEdit
```
from sklearn.preprocessing import PolynomialFeatures
from sklearn.pipeline import make_pipeline

# Creating polynomial regression model (degree=2)
poly_model = make_pipeline(PolynomialFeatures(degree=2),
LinearRegression())
poly_model.fit(X_train, y_train)

# Predictions
y_poly_pred = poly_model.predict(X_test)

# Visualizing Polynomial Regression
plt.scatter(df['Square_Feet'], df['Price'], color='blue',
label="Actual Prices")
plt.plot(X_test, y_poly_pred, color='red', linewidth=2,
label="Polynomial Fit")
plt.xlabel("Square Feet")
plt.ylabel("Price")
plt.legend()
plt.show()
```

When to Use Polynomial Regression?

- When data exhibits **curved relationships** rather than straight-line trends.

44

- Useful in **econometrics, engineering, and medical diagnostics**.

Ridge, Lasso, and Elastic Net Regression

When working with high-dimensional datasets, simple linear regression models may **overfit** the data, leading to poor generalization. **Regularization techniques** like Ridge, Lasso, and Elastic Net regression help in **reducing overfitting**.

6.3 Ridge Regression (L2 Regularization)

Ridge regression adds an **L2 penalty** (squared sum of coefficients) to the linear regression cost function:

$$\text{Loss} = \sum (Y - \hat{Y})^2 + \lambda \sum b_i^2$$

where λ **(lambda)** is the regularization parameter. Larger values of λ reduce overfitting by shrinking coefficients.

Example: Ridge Regression in Python
python
CopyEdit
```
from sklearn.linear_model import Ridge

ridge_model = Ridge(alpha=1.0)  # Adjust alpha to control
regularization strength
ridge_model.fit(X_train, y_train)
```

When to Use Ridge Regression?

- When dealing with **multicollinearity** (highly correlated features).
- When preventing overfitting in high-dimensional datasets.

6.4 Lasso Regression (L1 Regularization)

Lasso regression applies an **L1 penalty** (absolute sum of coefficients), which results in **feature selection** by setting some coefficients to **zero**:

$$\text{Loss} = \sum (Y - \hat{Y})^2 + \lambda \sum |b_i|$$

Example: Lasso Regression in Python
python
CopyEdit
```
from sklearn.linear_model import Lasso

lasso_model = Lasso(alpha=0.1)
lasso_model.fit(X_train, y_train)
```

When to Use Lasso Regression?

- When performing **feature selection** (eliminating irrelevant variables).
- When dealing with **sparse datasets**.

6.5 Elastic Net Regression (Combination of L1 & L2)

Elastic Net regression combines Ridge and Lasso penalties:

$$\text{Loss} = \sum (Y - \hat{Y})^2 + \lambda_1 \sum |b_i| + \lambda_2 \sum b_i^2$$

This balances **feature selection (Lasso)** and **coefficient shrinkage (Ridge)**.

Example: Elastic Net Regression in Python
python
CopyEdit
```
from sklearn.linear_model import ElasticNet

elastic_net_model = ElasticNet(alpha=0.1, l1_ratio=0.5)  #
l1_ratio balances Ridge vs. Lasso
```
46

```
elastic_net_model.fit(X_train, y_train)
```

When to Use Elastic Net Regression?

- When **Lasso alone selects too few features.**
- When **Ridge alone retains too many irrelevant features.**

Evaluating Regression Models (MSE, RMSE, R² Score)

Once a regression model is trained, it must be evaluated to measure its **performance** and **accuracy**.

6.6 Mean Squared Error (MSE)

Measures the average squared difference between actual and predicted values:

$$MSE = \frac{1}{n} \sum (Y - \hat{Y})^2$$

python
CopyEdit
```
from sklearn.metrics import mean_squared_error

mse = mean_squared_error(y_test, y_pred)
print("Mean Squared Error:", mse)
```

6.7 Root Mean Squared Error (RMSE)

RMSE is the square root of MSE, making it easier to interpret:

$$RMSE = \sqrt{MSE}$$

```python
CopyEdit
rmse = np.sqrt(mse)
print("Root Mean Squared Error:", rmse)
```

6.8 R² Score (Coefficient of Determination)

R² Score measures how well the model explains variance in the data:

$$R^2 = 1 - \frac{\sum(Y - \hat{Y})^2}{\sum(Y - \bar{Y})^2}$$

```python
CopyEdit
from sklearn.metrics import r2_score

r2 = r2_score(y_test, y_pred)
print("R² Score:", r2)
```

Interpretation:

- **R² = 1:** Perfect model.
- **R² > 0.75:** Strong predictive ability.
- **R² < 0.50:** Weak model.

Key Takeaways from Regression Models in AI

Concept	Usage in AI
Linear Regression	Predicts continuous trends (house prices, salaries)
Polynomial Regression	Models non-linear relationships

Ridge Regression	Prevents overfitting in high-dimensional data
Lasso Regression	Selects important features
Elastic Net Regression	Balances feature selection & regularization
MSE & RMSE	Measure prediction errors
R² Score	Evaluates model accuracy

By mastering these regression techniques, AI practitioners can build accurate predictive models for real-world applications. The next chapter will explore **classification algorithms for AI.**

Chapter 7

Classification Algorithms for AI

Classification is a fundamental technique in machine learning, used to categorize data into distinct groups. Unlike regression models that predict continuous values, classification models assign labels to data points. For example, classifying emails as spam or not spam, detecting fraudulent transactions, or identifying diseases based on symptoms.

This chapter will explore Logistic Regression, Decision Trees, Random Forest, Support Vector Machines (SVM), Naïve Bayes, and K-Nearest Neighbors (KNN). Additionally, we will cover model evaluation techniques, including the Confusion Matrix, Precision-Recall, and F1 Score.

Logistic Regression

7.1 What is Logistic Regression?

Logistic Regression is a simple yet powerful classification algorithm used for binary classification problems (e.g., predicting whether a tumor is malignant or benign). It estimates the probability that a given input belongs to a particular category using the sigmoid function:

$$P(Y = 1) = \frac{1}{1 + e^{-(b_0 + b_1 X_1 + b_2 X_2 + \cdots + b_n X_n)}}$$

The output probability is thresholded at 0.5:

- If P(Y=1)>0.5$P(Y=1) > 0.5$P(Y=1)>0.5, predict class 1.
- If P(Y=1)≤0.5$P(Y=1) \leq 0.5$P(Y=1)≤0.5, predict class 0.

7.2 Implementing Logistic Regression in Python

python

```python
from sklearn.linear_model import LogisticRegression

from sklearn.model_selection import train_test_split

from sklearn.metrics import accuracy_score


# Sample dataset

X = [[1], [2], [3], [4], [5], [6], [7], [8], [9]]

y = [0, 0, 0, 0, 1, 1, 1, 1, 1]  # Binary classification


# Splitting data

X_train, X_test, y_train, y_test = train_test_split(X, y,
test_size=0.2, random_state=42)


# Training Logistic Regression

model = LogisticRegression()

model.fit(X_train, y_train)


# Predictions

y_pred = model.predict(X_test)


# Accuracy

print("Accuracy:", accuracy_score(y_test, y_pred))
```

7.3 When to Use Logistic Regression?

- When the target variable is binary (0/1, True/False, Yes/No).
- When interpretability is important (e.g., medical diagnosis).
- When the dataset is linearly separable.

Decision Trees and Random Forest

8.1 Decision Trees

Decision Trees classify data by splitting it into branches based on feature conditions.

Example Decision Tree for Loan Approval:

1. Is the applicant's salary > $50,000?
   - Yes → Approved
   - No → Check Credit Score
2. Is the credit score > 700?
   - Yes → Approved
   - No → Rejected

Example: Decision Tree in Python

python

CopyEdit

```
from sklearn.tree import DecisionTreeClassifier


# Training a Decision Tree

tree_model = DecisionTreeClassifier(max_depth=3)

tree_model.fit(X_train, y_train)
```

8.2 Random Forest

Random Forest is an ensemble of multiple Decision Trees, which reduces overfitting and improves accuracy.

Example: Random Forest in Python

python

CopyEdit

```
from sklearn.ensemble import RandomForestClassifier


# Training a Random Forest Classifier

forest_model = RandomForestClassifier(n_estimators=100,
random_state=42)

forest_model.fit(X_train, y_train)
```

8.3 When to Use Decision Trees or Random Forest?

- Decision Trees work well for interpretable models.
- Random Forest is better for complex datasets and reduces overfitting.

Support Vector Machines (SVM)

9.1 What is SVM?

Support Vector Machines (SVM) classify data by finding the best decision boundary (hyperplane) that maximizes the margin between different classes.

9.2 Example: SVM in Python

python

CopyEdit

```
from sklearn.svm import SVC


# Training an SVM Classifier

svm_model = SVC(kernel="linear")

svm_model.fit(X_train, y_train)
```

9.3 When to Use SVM?

- When the data has clear separation between classes.
- When working with high-dimensional data (e.g., text classification).

Naïve Bayes and K-Nearest Neighbors (KNN)

10.1 Naïve Bayes Classifier

Naïve Bayes is a probabilistic classifier based on Bayes' Theorem:

$$P(A|B) = \frac{P(B|A)P(A)}{P(B)}$$

It is commonly used in text classification, such as spam detection.

Example: Naïve Bayes in Python

python

CopyEdit

```
from sklearn.naive_bayes import GaussianNB


# Training a Naïve Bayes Model
```

```
nb_model = GaussianNB()

nb_model.fit(X_train, y_train)
```

10.2 K-Nearest Neighbors (KNN)

KNN classifies new data points based on the majority class of its k-nearest neighbors.

Example: KNN in Python

python

CopyEdit

```
from sklearn.neighbors import KNeighborsClassifier


# Training a KNN Classifier

knn_model = KNeighborsClassifier(n_neighbors=5)

knn_model.fit(X_train, y_train)
```

10.3 When to Use Naïve Bayes or KNN?

Algorithm	Best Use Case
Naïve Bayes	Spam filtering, sentiment analysis
KNN	Image recognition, recommendation systems

Model Evaluation (Confusion Matrix, Precision-Recall, F1 Score)

11.1 Confusion Matrix

A Confusion Matrix evaluates classification performance:

	Predicted Positive	Predicted Negative
Actual Positive	True Positive (TP)	False Negative (FN)
Actual Negative	False Positive (FP)	True Negative (TN)

Example: Confusion Matrix in Python

python

CopyEdit

```
from sklearn.metrics import confusion_matrix


# Compute Confusion Matrix
```

```
cm = confusion_matrix(y_test, y_pred)

print(cm)
```

11.2 Precision, Recall, and F1 Score

Metric	Formula	Interpretation
Precision	$$Precision = \frac{TP}{TP + FP}$$	How many predicted positives were actually correct?
Recall (Sensitivity)	$$Recall = \frac{TP}{TP + FN}$$	How many actual positives were correctly predicted?
F1 Score	$$F1 = 2 \times \frac{Precision \times Recall}{Precision + Recall}$$	Balance between Precision & Recall

Example: Computing Precision, Recall, and F1 Score

python

CopyEdit

```
from sklearn.metrics import precision_score, recall_score,
f1_score
```

```
print("Precision:", precision_score(y_test, y_pred))

print("Recall:", recall_score(y_test, y_pred))

print("F1 Score:", f1_score(y_test, y_pred))
```

Key Takeaways from Classification Algorithms in AI

Algorithm	Best Use Case
Logistic Regression	Binary classification (disease detection, fraud detection)
Decision Trees	Explainable AI, customer segmentation
Random Forest	Large, complex datasets (fraud detection, medical diagnosis)
SVM	Text classification, facial recognition
Naïve Bayes	Sentiment analysis, spam detection
KNN	Pattern recognition, recommendation systems

Classification algorithms power AI-driven decision-making systems, from predictive analytics to real-time fraud detection. The next chapter will explore Unsupervised Learning techniques such as Clustering and Dimensionality Reduction.`

Chapter 8

Clustering Techniques

Clustering is a core concept in unsupervised learning, where the goal is to group similar data points without predefined labels. Unlike supervised learning, where models learn from labeled data, clustering algorithms discover hidden patterns and structures in data, making them invaluable for tasks like customer segmentation, anomaly detection, and image compression.

This chapter explores three powerful clustering algorithms:

- K-Means Clustering – A simple and efficient partitioning method.
- Hierarchical Clustering – Builds a hierarchy of clusters.
- DBSCAN (Density-Based Spatial Clustering of Applications with Noise) – Detects arbitrary-shaped clusters and anomalies.

K-Means Clustering

8.1 What is K-Means?

K-Means is a centroid-based clustering algorithm that partitions data into K distinct clusters, where each cluster is defined by a centroid (mean position of points in that cluster).

8.2 How K-Means Works

The algorithm follows these steps:

1. Initialize K Centroids – Randomly select KKK data points as the initial cluster centers.
2. Assign Points to the Nearest Centroid – Compute the distance of each point to all centroids and assign it to the closest one.
3. Update Centroids – Compute the mean of all points in each cluster and move the centroid to this mean.
4. Repeat Until Convergence – Steps 2 and 3 are repeated until centroids no longer change.

8.3 Example: K-Means in Python

python

CopyEdit

```python
import numpy as np

import matplotlib.pyplot as plt

from sklearn.cluster import KMeans

from sklearn.datasets import make_blobs


# Generating synthetic dataset

X, _ = make_blobs(n_samples=300, centers=3, cluster_std=1.0,
random_state=42)


# Applying K-Means

kmeans = KMeans(n_clusters=3, random_state=42)

kmeans.fit(X)

y_kmeans = kmeans.predict(X)


# Plot clusters

plt.scatter(X[:, 0], X[:, 1], c=y_kmeans, cmap='viridis',
alpha=0.5)

plt.scatter(kmeans.cluster_centers_[:, 0],
kmeans.cluster_centers_[:, 1], s=300, c='red', marker='x')

plt.title("K-Means Clustering")
```

```
plt.show()
```

8.4 Choosing the Right K (Elbow Method)

The Elbow Method helps determine the optimal number of clusters by plotting the Sum of Squared Errors (SSE) for different values of KKK. The ideal KKK is where SSE stops decreasing sharply.

python

CopyEdit

```
sse = []

for k in range(1, 11):

    kmeans = KMeans(n_clusters=k, random_state=42)

    kmeans.fit(X)

    sse.append(kmeans.inertia_)


plt.plot(range(1, 11), sse, marker='o')

plt.xlabel("Number of Clusters (K)")

plt.ylabel("SSE")

plt.title("Elbow Method for Optimal K")

plt.show()
```

8.5 When to Use K-Means?

When clusters are spherical and evenly sized.
When scalability is important (K-Means is computationally efficient).
Not ideal for arbitrarily shaped or overlapping clusters.

61

Hierarchical Clustering

9.1 What is Hierarchical Clustering?

Hierarchical clustering builds a tree-like hierarchy of clusters that allows for visualization of relationships between data points. It comes in two forms:

1. Agglomerative Clustering (Bottom-Up) – Each data point starts as its own cluster, and clusters are merged iteratively.
2. Divisive Clustering (Top-Down) – Starts with a single cluster containing all data points and recursively splits into smaller clusters.

9.2 How Agglomerative Clustering Works

1. Calculate Distance Matrix – Compute distances between all points.
2. Merge Closest Clusters – Find two clusters that are closest and merge them.
3. Repeat Until a Single Cluster Remains – The process continues until all points belong to one cluster.

9.3 Example: Hierarchical Clustering in Python

python

CopyEdit

```
import scipy.cluster.hierarchy as sch

from sklearn.cluster import AgglomerativeClustering


# Generating dataset

X, _ = make_blobs(n_samples=300, centers=4, cluster_std=1.0,
random_state=42)


# Plot dendrogram
```

```python
plt.figure(figsize=(10, 5))

dendrogram = sch.dendrogram(sch.linkage(X, method='ward'))

plt.title("Dendrogram")

plt.xlabel("Data Points")

plt.ylabel("Euclidean Distance")

plt.show()


# Apply Agglomerative Clustering

hc = AgglomerativeClustering(n_clusters=4, affinity='euclidean',
linkage='ward')

y_hc = hc.fit_predict(X)


# Plot clusters

plt.scatter(X[:, 0], X[:, 1], c=y_hc, cmap='viridis', alpha=0.5)

plt.title("Agglomerative Hierarchical Clustering")

plt.show()
```

9.4 Pros and Cons of Hierarchical Clustering

No need to specify KKK beforehand (can determine clusters from the dendrogram).
Works well with small to medium-sized datasets.
Computationally expensive for large datasets.

DBSCAN Algorithm (Density-Based Clustering)

10.1 What is DBSCAN?

DBSCAN (Density-Based Spatial Clustering of Applications with Noise) groups dense areas of data while identifying outliers as noise. Unlike K-Means and hierarchical clustering, DBSCAN does not require specifying the number of clusters (K).

10.2 How DBSCAN Works

1. Define Core Points – Points with at least MinPts neighbors within radius Epsilon (ε) are considered core points.
2. Expand Clusters – Core points expand by adding all reachable points.
3. Label Outliers – Points that do not belong to any cluster are classified as noise.

10.3 Example: DBSCAN in Python

python

CopyEdit

```
from sklearn.cluster import DBSCAN


# Applying DBSCAN

dbscan = DBSCAN(eps=0.5, min_samples=5)

y_dbscan = dbscan.fit_predict(X)


# Plot clusters

plt.scatter(X[:, 0], X[:, 1], c=y_dbscan, cmap='viridis',
alpha=0.5)

plt.title("DBSCAN Clustering")

plt.show()
```

10.4 Choosing DBSCAN Parameters (ε and MinPts)

- Epsilon (ε) – The neighborhood radius around each point.
- MinPts – The minimum number of points required to form a dense region.

10.5 When to Use DBSCAN?

Detects arbitrarily shaped clusters.
Identifies outliers automatically.
Not ideal for datasets with varying densities.

Comparing Clustering Techniques

Algorithm	Strengths	Weaknesses
K-Means	Fast, easy to implement	Assumes spherical clusters, sensitive to outliers
Hierarchical Clustering	No need to specify K, interpretable dendrogram	Computationally expensive for large datasets
DBSCAN	Handles noise, detects irregular shapes	Struggles with varying densities

---

Key Takeaways from Clustering Techniques

- K-Means is efficient for well-defined clusters but struggles with non-spherical data.
- Hierarchical Clustering does not require predefining K but is computationally expensive for large datasets.
- DBSCAN is ideal for density-based clustering and outlier detection but struggles with varying densities.

Clustering is a powerful unsupervised learning technique that helps discover hidden patterns in data, providing insights for customer segmentation, anomaly detection, and recommendation systems. The next chapter will explore dimensionality reduction techniques like PCA and t-SNE, which help visualize and preprocess high-dimensional data for AI models.

Chapter 9

Dimensionality Reduction

In artificial intelligence and machine learning, high-dimensional data can lead to computational inefficiency, overfitting, and difficulties in visualization. Many AI models struggle with the curse of dimensionality, where an increasing number of features reduces model performance. Dimensionality reduction techniques help address this problem by reducing the number of input features while preserving essential information.

This chapter explores three key dimensionality reduction techniques:

- Principal Component Analysis (PCA) – A widely used linear method for feature reduction.
- t-Distributed Stochastic Neighbor Embedding (t-SNE) – A nonlinear technique for visualization of high-dimensional data.
- Autoencoders – Neural networks used for learning compact feature representations.

Principal Component Analysis (PCA)

9.1 What is PCA?

Principal Component Analysis (PCA) is a linear dimensionality reduction technique that transforms high-dimensional data into a lower-dimensional space while preserving variance.

Key concepts in PCA:

- Principal Components (PCs): New variables that are linear combinations of original features.
- Eigenvalues & Eigenvectors: Determine the importance of each PC.
- Variance Explained: Higher variance indicates more information retained.

9.2 How PCA Works

1. Standardize the data (mean = 0, variance = 1).

2. Compute covariance matrix to identify relationships between features.
3. Perform Eigen decomposition on the covariance matrix to find principal components.
4. Select top kkk components that explain the most variance.
5. Transform data into the new subspace.

9.3 Implementing PCA in Python

python

CopyEdit

```
import numpy as np

import matplotlib.pyplot as plt

import pandas as pd

from sklearn.decomposition import PCA

from sklearn.preprocessing import StandardScaler

from sklearn.datasets import load_digits


# Load dataset

digits = load_digits()

X = digits.data


# Standardizing the data

scaler = StandardScaler()

X_scaled = scaler.fit_transform(X)


# Apply PCA to reduce dimensions to 2
```

```
pca = PCA(n_components=2)

X_pca = pca.fit_transform(X_scaled)


# Plot PCA result

plt.scatter(X_pca[:, 0], X_pca[:, 1], c=digits.target,
cmap="viridis", alpha=0.5)

plt.xlabel("Principal Component 1")

plt.ylabel("Principal Component 2")

plt.title("PCA Visualization of Digits Dataset")

plt.colorbar()

plt.show()
```

9.4 Choosing the Optimal Number of Components

To decide the number of components to retain, we use an explained variance plot:

python

CopyEdit

```
pca_full = PCA()

pca_full.fit(X_scaled)


plt.plot(np.cumsum(pca_full.explained_variance_ratio_),
marker='o')

plt.xlabel("Number of Principal Components")

plt.ylabel("Cumulative Explained Variance")
```

```
plt.title("Choosing the Number of Components")

plt.show()
```

9.5 When to Use PCA?

When reducing high-dimensional datasets for efficiency.
When avoiding multicollinearity in data.
When improving AI model performance by removing redundant features.
Not ideal for nonlinear data (use t-SNE instead).

t-Distributed Stochastic Neighbor Embedding (t-SNE)

10.1 What is t-SNE?

t-SNE (t-Distributed Stochastic Neighbor Embedding) is a nonlinear dimensionality reduction technique that maps high-dimensional data into 2D or 3D space for visualization.

Unlike PCA, t-SNE preserves local structure in data, making it ideal for visualizing clusters in complex datasets.

10.2 How t-SNE Works

1. Compute pairwise similarity between high-dimensional data points.
2. Map points into low-dimensional space while maintaining pairwise similarities.
3. Optimize embeddings using gradient descent.

10.3 Implementing t-SNE in Python

python

CopyEdit

```
from sklearn.manifold import TSNE


# Apply t-SNE to reduce to 2D

tsne = TSNE(n_components=2, random_state=42)
```

```
X_tsne = tsne.fit_transform(X_scaled)

# Plot t-SNE result

plt.scatter(X_tsne[:, 0], X_tsne[:, 1], c=digits.target,
cmap="viridis", alpha=0.5)

plt.xlabel("t-SNE Component 1")

plt.ylabel("t-SNE Component 2")

plt.title("t-SNE Visualization of Digits Dataset")

plt.colorbar()

plt.show()
```

10.4 PCA vs. t-SNE: When to Use Which?

Criteria	PCA	t-SNE
Type	Linear	Nonlinear
Goal	Reduce dimensions while preserving variance	Preserve local structures for visualization
Scalability	Works well for large datasets	Computationally expensive for large datasets
Visualization	Not ideal for complex data	Excellent for complex datasets with clusters

Use PCA for feature reduction in machine learning models.
Use t-SNE for visualizing high-dimensional data clusters.

Autoencoders for Feature Reduction

11.1 What are Autoencoders?

Autoencoders are a type of neural network used for unsupervised feature learning and dimensionality reduction.

An autoencoder consists of:

- Encoder: Compresses input data into a smaller representation.
- Bottleneck (Latent Space): Stores compressed information.
- Decoder: Reconstructs the original data from the compressed representation.

11.2 How Autoencoders Work

1. Input data is passed through the encoder.
2. The encoder compresses the data into a low-dimensional representation.
3. The decoder reconstructs the original data from the compressed representation.
4. The model learns by minimizing reconstruction loss.

11.3 Implementing an Autoencoder in Python

python

CopyEdit

```
import tensorflow as tf

from tensorflow.keras.models import Model

from tensorflow.keras.layers import Input, Dense


# Define input layer

input_dim = X_scaled.shape[1]

input_layer = Input(shape=(input_dim,))


# Encoder
```

```python
encoded = Dense(64, activation="relu")(input_layer)

encoded = Dense(32, activation="relu")(encoded)

encoded = Dense(16, activation="relu")(encoded)


# Decoder

decoded = Dense(32, activation="relu")(encoded)

decoded = Dense(64, activation="relu")(decoded)

decoded = Dense(input_dim, activation="sigmoid")(decoded)


# Build autoencoder model

autoencoder = Model(input_layer, decoded)

autoencoder.compile(optimizer="adam", loss="mse")


# Train autoencoder

autoencoder.fit(X_scaled, X_scaled, epochs=50, batch_size=32,
shuffle=True, verbose=1)
```

11.4 Extracting Features from Autoencoders

python

CopyEdit

```python
encoder = Model(input_layer, encoded)   # Extract compressed
features

X_reduced = encoder.predict(X_scaled)
```

11.5 When to Use Autoencoders?

When working with nonlinear and complex datasets.
When performing feature extraction for deep learning models.
When handling high-dimensional data in unsupervised learning.
Not ideal for small datasets (requires large training data).

Key Takeaways from Dimensionality Reduction Techniques

Technique	Best Use Case
PCA	Feature reduction for machine learning models
t-SNE	Visualizing high-dimensional clusters
Autoencoders	Unsupervised feature learning for deep learning

By using these techniques, AI practitioners can improve model efficiency, reduce overfitting, and visualize high-dimensional data effectively. The next chapter will delve into Deep Learning and Neural Networks, covering how AI models learn from data.

Chapter 10

Introduction to Deep Learning

Deep learning has revolutionized artificial intelligence (AI) by enabling machines to learn complex patterns from data with minimal human intervention. It powers applications like image recognition, natural language processing (NLP), self-driving cars, and medical diagnostics. Unlike traditional machine learning, which often relies on hand-engineered features, deep learning uses neural networks that automatically extract relevant features from raw data.

This chapter introduces neural networks, covering perceptrons, activation functions, backpropagation, and gradient descent, the core mechanisms that enable deep learning models to learn from data.

Neural Networks Basics (Perceptrons, Activation Functions)

10.1 What is a Neural Network?

A neural network is a computational model inspired by the human brain. It consists of interconnected processing units called neurons, which process information and make decisions.

Structure of a Neural Network:

- Input Layer – Receives raw data (e.g., pixels in an image).
- Hidden Layers – Perform computations and extract patterns.
- Output Layer – Produces predictions (e.g., classifies an image as cat or dog).

10.2 Perceptrons: The Building Block of Neural Networks

The simplest neural network is a perceptron, modeled after biological neurons. It takes multiple inputs, applies weights, sums them, and passes the result through an activation function to produce an output.

Mathematical Representation of a Perceptron

$$Y = f(W_1X_1 + W_2X_2 + \dots + W_nX_n + b)$$

Where:

- X1,X2,...,XnX_1, X_2, ..., X_nX1,X2,...,Xn are input features.
- W1,W2,...,WnW_1, W_2, ..., W_nW1,W2,...,Wn are weights.
- bbb is the bias (adjusts output).
- fff is the activation function.
- YYY is the output.

Example: Perceptron in Python

python

CopyEdit

```
import numpy as np


# Define inputs and weights

X = np.array([0.5, 0.8])   # Inputs

W = np.array([0.4, 0.6])   # Weights

b = 0.1   # Bias


# Compute weighted sum

output = np.dot(W, X) + b

print("Perceptron Output:", output)
```

10.3 Activation Functions: Adding Non-Linearity

Without activation functions, neural networks would behave like linear models. Activation functions introduce non-linearity, allowing the network to learn complex relationships.

Common Activation Functions:

Activation Function	Formula	Usage
Sigmoid	$f(x) = \dfrac{1}{1 + e^{-x}}$	Binary classification
ReLU (Rectified Linear Unit)	$f(x) = \max(0, x)$	Most deep learning models
Tanh (Hyperbolic Tangent)	$f(x) = \dfrac{e^x - e^{-x}}{e^x + e^{-x}}$	Better than sigmoid for hidden layers
Softmax	$f(x_i) = \dfrac{e^{x_i}}{\sum e^{x_j}}$	Multi-class classification

Example: Using ReLU Activation in Python

python

CopyEdit

```
def relu(x):
    return max(0, x)


print(relu(-2))  # Output: 0

print(relu(3))   # Output: 3
```

10.4 Multi-Layer Perceptron (MLP)

A single-layer perceptron can only solve simple problems like AND/OR gates. For complex tasks like image recognition, we use a multi-layer perceptron (MLP) with multiple hidden layers.

Example: Neural Network with 2 Hidden Layers

python

CopyEdit

```python
from tensorflow.keras.models import Sequential

from tensorflow.keras.layers import Dense


# Define MLP Model

model = Sequential([

    Dense(32, activation='relu', input_shape=(10,)),  # First
hidden layer

    Dense(16, activation='relu'),  # Second hidden layer

    Dense(1, activation='sigmoid')  # Output layer (binary
classification)

])


# Compile the model

model.compile(optimizer='adam', loss='binary_crossentropy',
metrics=['accuracy'])

print(model.summary())
```

Understanding Backpropagation and Gradient Descent

11.1 What is Backpropagation?

Backpropagation (Backward Propagation of Errors) is the learning process that allows neural networks to adjust their weights to minimize errors.

How Backpropagation Works:

1. Forward Pass – The input propagates through the network to produce an output.
2. Compute Loss – The difference between predicted and actual values is calculated.
3. Backward Pass – Errors are propagated backward to update weights.
4. Weight Adjustment – Weights are updated using gradient descent to minimize the loss.

11.2 Gradient Descent: Optimizing Neural Networks

Gradient Descent is the optimization algorithm that adjusts weights to reduce loss. It updates weights in the direction that minimizes the error.

Gradient Descent Formula:

$$W = W - \alpha \frac{dL}{dW}$$

Key Fixes:

1. **Fraction formatting**: Used $\frac{dL}{dW}$ correctly.

2. **Removed redundant repetitions**: Ensured clarity in the formula.

Explanation:

- W: Current weight parameter.

- α (Learning Rate): Controls the step size in the weight update.

- $\frac{dL}{dW}$ (Gradient): Represents the rate of change of the loss function L with respect to weight W.

- **The formula updates the weight by moving it in the direction that minimizes the loss**, making it a core concept in optimization for machine learning.

11.3 Types of Gradient Descent

Type	Description	Pros	Cons
Batch Gradient Descent	Uses the entire dataset to compute gradients	Stable convergence	Slow for large datasets
Stochastic Gradient Descent (SGD)	Updates weights after each sample	Faster training	Noisy updates
Mini-Batch Gradient Descent	Updates weights using small batches	Balance between efficiency and stability	Requires tuning batch size

Example: Implementing Gradient Descent in Python

python

CopyEdit

```python
# Simulating simple gradient descent

def gradient_descent(w, learning_rate, gradient):
    return w - learning_rate * gradient


# Example update

w = 0.5  # Initial weight
```

```python
gradient = 0.1  # Example gradient

learning_rate = 0.01  # Step size


new_w = gradient_descent(w, learning_rate, gradient)

print("Updated Weight:", new_w)
```

11.4 Optimization Algorithms in Deep Learning

In deep learning, advanced optimization algorithms improve convergence speed:

Optimizer	Description
SGD (Stochastic Gradient Descent)	Basic optimization method
Adam (Adaptive Moment Estimation)	Combines momentum with adaptive learning rates (widely used)
RMSprop (Root Mean Square Propagation)	Works well with recurrent networks
Adagrad	Adjusts learning rates based on past gradients

Example: Using Adam Optimizer in a Neural Network

python

81

```
model.compile(optimizer='adam', loss='binary_crossentropy',
metrics=['accuracy'])
```

Key Takeaways from Deep Learning Basics

Concept	Importance
Neural Networks	Mimic the human brain to solve AI problems
Activation Functions	Introduce non-linearity for learning complex patterns
Backpropagation	Enables learning by updating weights using gradients
Gradient Descent	Optimizes model performance by minimizing loss
Optimizers (Adam, SGD, RMSprop)	Improve training efficiency and stability

Neural networks form the backbone of modern AI systems. The next chapter will cover building deep learning models using TensorFlow and PyTorch, allowing us to apply these concepts in real-world AI applications.

Chapter 11

Building Neural Networks with TensorFlow & PyTorch

Deep learning frameworks like TensorFlow and PyTorch have revolutionized AI development, making it easier to design, train, and deploy neural networks. These frameworks provide automatic differentiation, GPU acceleration, and high-level APIs, enabling rapid experimentation.

This chapter covers:

- Setting Up Neural Networks with TensorFlow – Defining, compiling, and training models.
- Training and Tuning Deep Learning Models – Hyperparameter tuning and model optimization.
- PyTorch for Dynamic Neural Networks – Leveraging PyTorch's flexibility for advanced architectures.

Setting Up Neural Networks with TensorFlow

11.1 Introduction to TensorFlow

TensorFlow is an open-source deep learning library developed by Google. It is widely used for image recognition, natural language processing, and AI automation.

Supports both low-level operations (TensorFlow Core API) and high-level APIs (Keras). Efficient GPU acceleration for large-scale training.
Used in Google AI products like Google Translate and DeepMind.

11.2 Installing TensorFlow

To install TensorFlow, use:

bash

CopyEdit

```
pip install tensorflow
```

Verify installation:

python

CopyEdit

```python
import tensorflow as tf

print(tf.__version__)  # Check TensorFlow version
```

11.3 Building a Neural Network with TensorFlow (Using Keras API)

TensorFlow provides the Keras API, which makes defining neural networks intuitive.

Step 1: Import Required Libraries

python

CopyEdit

```python
import tensorflow as tf

from tensorflow.keras.models import Sequential

from tensorflow.keras.layers import Dense, Flatten
```

Step 2: Define the Neural Network Architecture

python

CopyEdit

```python
model = Sequential([

    Dense(128, activation='relu', input_shape=(10,)),  # Input
layer with 10 features

    Dense(64, activation='relu'),  # Hidden layer
```

```
    Dense(1, activation='sigmoid')  # Output layer (binary
classification)

])
```

Step 3: Compile the Model

python

CopyEdit

```
model.compile(optimizer='adam', loss='binary_crossentropy',
metrics=['accuracy'])
```

Step 4: Train the Model

python

CopyEdit

```
import numpy as np


# Generate synthetic data

X_train = np.random.rand(1000, 10)

y_train = np.random.randint(2, size=1000)


# Train the model

model.fit(X_train, y_train, epochs=10, batch_size=32)
```

Step 5: Evaluate the Model

python

CopyEdit

```python
X_test = np.random.rand(200, 10)

y_test = np.random.randint(2, size=200)


loss, accuracy = model.evaluate(X_test, y_test)

print(f"Test Accuracy: {accuracy:.2f}")
```

Training and Tuning Deep Learning Models

Training deep learning models involves optimizing hyperparameters like learning rate, batch size, and number of layers.

11.4 Hyperparameter Tuning

Hyperparameter tuning is essential to improve model performance. Key hyperparameters to tune include:

Hyperparameter	Description	Common Values
Learning Rate	Controls weight updates	0.001, 0.0001
Batch Size	Number of samples per training step	32, 64, 128

Number of Layers	Depth of the network	2-10
Number of Neurons	Units per hidden layer	64, 128, 256

Example: Grid Search for Hyperparameter Tuning

python

CopyEdit

```python
from tensorflow.keras.wrappers.scikit_learn import
KerasClassifier

from sklearn.model_selection import GridSearchCV


def create_model(optimizer='adam'):

    model = Sequential([

        Dense(64, activation='relu', input_shape=(10,)),

        Dense(1, activation='sigmoid')

    ])

    model.compile(optimizer=optimizer,
loss='binary_crossentropy', metrics=['accuracy'])

    return model


# Wrap model for use in GridSearch

model = KerasClassifier(build_fn=create_model, verbose=0)
```

```python
param_grid = {'optimizer': ['adam', 'sgd']}

grid = GridSearchCV(estimator=model, param_grid=param_grid,
cv=3)

grid.fit(X_train, y_train)


print("Best Parameters:", grid.best_params_)
```

11.5 Using Callbacks for Early Stopping and Learning Rate Adjustment

TensorFlow provides callbacks to automatically stop training if the model stops improving.

Early Stopping to Prevent Overfitting

python

CopyEdit

```python
from tensorflow.keras.callbacks import EarlyStopping


early_stopping = EarlyStopping(monitor='val_loss', patience=5,
restore_best_weights=True)


model.fit(X_train, y_train, epochs=50, batch_size=32,
validation_split=0.2, callbacks=[early_stopping])
```

Reduce Learning Rate on Plateau

python

```
from tensorflow.keras.callbacks import ReduceLROnPlateau


lr_scheduler = ReduceLROnPlateau(monitor='val_loss', factor=0.5,
patience=3)

model.fit(X_train, y_train, epochs=50, batch_size=32,
validation_split=0.2, callbacks=[lr_scheduler])
```

PyTorch for Dynamic Neural Networks

11.6 Introduction to PyTorch

PyTorch, developed by Meta (Facebook AI), is known for its flexibility and ease of debugging.

Supports dynamic computation graphs (easier debugging).
Provides tensor computation similar to NumPy.
Used by research teams in OpenAI, DeepMind, and Tesla Autopilot.

11.7 Installing PyTorch

To install PyTorch, use:

bash

```
pip install torch torchvision
```

Verify installation:

python

```
import torch

print(torch.__version__)  # Check PyTorch version
```

11.8 Building a Neural Network with PyTorch

Unlike TensorFlow, PyTorch uses explicit class-based model definitions.

Step 1: Define the Model

python

```
import torch.nn as nn

import torch.optim as optim


class NeuralNetwork(nn.Module):

    def __init__(self):

        super(NeuralNetwork, self).__init__()

        self.fc1 = nn.Linear(10, 128)

        self.fc2 = nn.Linear(128, 64)

        self.fc3 = nn.Linear(64, 1)

        self.sigmoid = nn.Sigmoid()


    def forward(self, x):
```

```
        x = torch.relu(self.fc1(x))

        x = torch.relu(self.fc2(x))

        x = self.sigmoid(self.fc3(x))

        return x


# Instantiate the model

model = NeuralNetwork()
```

Step 2: Define Loss Function and Optimizer

python

CopyEdit

```
criterion = nn.BCELoss()  # Binary Cross-Entropy Loss

optimizer = optim.Adam(model.parameters(), lr=0.001)
```

Step 3: Training the Model

python

CopyEdit

```
X_train_tensor = torch.tensor(X_train, dtype=torch.float32)

y_train_tensor = torch.tensor(y_train,
dtype=torch.float32).view(-1, 1)


for epoch in range(10):

    optimizer.zero_grad()  # Reset gradients
```

```
outputs = model(X_train_tensor)  # Forward pass

loss = criterion(outputs, y_train_tensor)  # Compute loss

loss.backward()  # Backpropagation

optimizer.step()  # Update weights

print(f"Epoch {epoch+1}, Loss: {loss.item():.4f}")
```

Step 4: Evaluating the Model

python

CopyEdit

```
X_test_tensor = torch.tensor(X_test, dtype=torch.float32)

y_test_tensor = torch.tensor(y_test,
dtype=torch.float32).view(-1, 1)


with torch.no_grad():

    y_pred = model(X_test_tensor)

    accuracy = ((y_pred > 0.5).float() ==
y_test_tensor).float().mean()

    print(f"Test Accuracy: {accuracy:.2f}")
```

Key Takeaways from TensorFlow & PyTorch

Framework	Best Use Case

TensorFlow	Production deployment, large-scale AI applications
PyTorch	Research, flexible deep learning experiments
Keras (TensorFlow API)	Rapid prototyping, beginner-friendly development

Both TensorFlow and PyTorch are powerful for deep learning. The next chapter will dive into Convolutional Neural Networks (CNNs), a specialized architecture for image recognition and computer vision tasks.

Chapter 12

Convolutional Neural Networks (CNNs) for Image Recognition

Image recognition is one of the most prominent applications of deep learning, powering technologies like facial recognition, medical image analysis, and self-driving cars. Traditional neural networks struggle with image data due to their inability to capture spatial hierarchies and local features effectively.

Convolutional Neural Networks (CNNs) solve this problem by using specialized layers that extract patterns from images, making them the backbone of computer vision applications.

This chapter covers:

- CNN Architecture (Convolution, Pooling, Fully Connected Layers) – Understanding the key building blocks of CNNs.
- Training a CNN for Image Classification – Implementing and training a CNN in Python using TensorFlow.

CNN Architecture (Convolution, Pooling, Fully Connected Layers)

12.1 How CNNs Work

A Convolutional Neural Network (CNN) is designed to automatically and adaptively learn spatial hierarchies of features from images. Unlike traditional deep networks, CNNs preserve spatial relationships by using filters that detect edges, textures, and objects.

The standard CNN architecture consists of three main components:

1. Convolutional Layers – Extract patterns like edges, textures, and shapes.
2. Pooling Layers – Reduce the spatial dimensions while retaining key features.
3. Fully Connected Layers – Interpret extracted features and make predictions.

12.2 Convolutional Layers

The Convolutional Layer applies a set of filters (kernels) to the input image, sliding across it to detect patterns.

Mathematical Representation

$$O(i, j) = \sum W \cdot X + B$$

Key Fixes:

1. **Proper summation notation:** Used $\sum W \cdot X$ correctly.

2. **Removed redundant repetitions:** Ensured clarity in the formula.

Explanation:

- $O(i, j)$: The output pixel value at position (i, j) in the feature map.

- W: The filter (also called kernel), which extracts patterns from the input image.

- X: The input image or feature map being processed.

- B: The bias term, which adjusts the output.

- The **convolution operation** slides the kernel over the image, computing weighted sums of pixel

Example: Applying a Convolutional Filter

A 3x3 filter applied to an image matrix:

Input Image (3x3)	Filter (Kernel)	Output
1 2 3	0 1 0	6
4 5 6	1 -4 1	-5
7 8 9	0 1 0	6

Filters help detect edges, textures, and patterns automatically.

12.3 Pooling Layers

Pooling layers reduce the spatial dimensions of feature maps while retaining important information, making the model computationally efficient.

Type of Pooling	Operation
Max Pooling	Takes the maximum value in each region (preserves dominant features).
Average Pooling	Takes the average value in each region (smoothens features).

Example: Max Pooling (2x2 Filter)

Input (4x4)	Max Pooled (2x2)
1 3 2 4	3 4
5 6 7 8	6 8
9 10 11 12	10 12
13 14 15 16	14 16

Max pooling reduces computation while keeping important image details.

12.4 Fully Connected Layers (FC Layers)

After convolution and pooling, the extracted features are flattened into a one-dimensional vector and passed through fully connected (dense) layers for final classification.

$$\text{Prediction} = W_1 X_1 + W_2 X_2 + ... + W_n X_n + B$$

Training a CNN for Image Classification

12.5 Dataset for Image Classification

To train a CNN, we need an image dataset. The CIFAR-10 dataset is commonly used, containing 60,000 images of 10 object categories (e.g., airplane, car, dog, cat).

12.6 Implementing a CNN with TensorFlow

Step 1: Import Libraries

python

CopyEdit

```
import tensorflow as tf

from tensorflow.keras import layers, models

import matplotlib.pyplot as plt

from tensorflow.keras.datasets import cifar10

import numpy as np
```

Step 2: Load and Preprocess CIFAR-10 Dataset

python

CopyEdit

```
# Load dataset

(X_train, y_train), (X_test, y_test) = cifar10.load_data()


# Normalize pixel values between 0 and 1

X_train, X_test = X_train / 255.0, X_test / 255.0


# Print dataset shape

print("Training set shape:", X_train.shape)

print("Test set shape:", X_test.shape)
```

12.7 Define CNN Architecture

python

CopyEdit

```
# Define CNN model

model = models.Sequential([

    layers.Conv2D(32, (3,3), activation='relu', input_shape=(32, 32, 3)),  # Convolution Layer

    layers.MaxPooling2D((2,2)),  # Max Pooling Layer

    layers.Conv2D(64, (3,3), activation='relu'),
```

```
    layers.MaxPooling2D((2,2)),

    layers.Conv2D(128, (3,3), activation='relu'),

    layers.Flatten(),   # Convert 2D features into 1D

    layers.Dense(128, activation='relu'),   # Fully Connected
Layer

    layers.Dense(10, activation='softmax')   # Output Layer (10
classes)

])
```

```
# Compile the model

model.compile(optimizer='adam',
loss='sparse_categorical_crossentropy', metrics=['accuracy'])
```

12.8 Train the CNN Model

python

CopyEdit

```
# Train the model

model.fit(X_train, y_train, epochs=10, batch_size=64,
validation_data=(X_test, y_test))
```

12.9 Evaluate Model Performance

python

CopyEdit

```
# Evaluate test accuracy

test_loss, test_acc = model.evaluate(X_test, y_test)
```

```python
print(f"Test Accuracy: {test_acc:.2f}")
```

12.10 Visualizing Model Performance

python

CopyEdit

```python
# Plot sample predictions
fig, axes = plt.subplots(1, 5, figsize=(10, 3))
class_names = ["Airplane", "Automobile", "Bird", "Cat", "Deer",
                "Dog", "Frog", "Horse", "Ship", "Truck"]


for i, ax in enumerate(axes):
    ax.imshow(X_test[i])
    ax.set_title(f"Label: {class_names[y_test[i][0]]}")
    ax.axis("off")
plt.show()
```

12.11 Improving CNN Performance

To further improve CNN performance, we can use:
Data Augmentation: Applying rotations, flips, and zooms to increase dataset variability.
Batch Normalization: Normalizing activations for faster convergence.
Transfer Learning: Using pre-trained CNN models like ResNet, VGG16, MobileNet.

Example: Adding Data Augmentation

python

CopyEdit

```python
from tensorflow.keras.preprocessing.image import
ImageDataGenerator
```

```
datagen = ImageDataGenerator(rotation_range=20,
horizontal_flip=True)

datagen.fit(X_train)
```

Key Takeaways from CNNs for Image Recognition

Component	Purpose
Convolutional Layers	Extract image features (edges, textures, shapes).
Pooling Layers	Reduce dimensions while retaining essential patterns.
Fully Connected Layers	Make final classifications based on extracted features.
Data Augmentation	Improves generalization by creating variations of training data.

CNNs have revolutionized image recognition, making AI better at tasks like medical imaging, self-driving cars, and facial recognition. The next chapter will explore Recurrent Neural Networks (RNNs) and Transformers for Natural Language Processing (NLP), which specialize in processing sequential data like text and speech.

Chapter 13

Recurrent Neural Networks (RNNs) & Transformers for NLP

Deep learning has revolutionized Natural Language Processing (NLP) and time-series prediction through specialized architectures that process sequential data. Unlike standard neural networks, which assume all inputs are independent, Recurrent Neural Networks (RNNs), Long Short-Term Memory Networks (LSTMs), and Gated Recurrent Units (GRUs) are designed to capture relationships across time.

More recently, Transformers like BERT (Bidirectional Encoder Representations from Transformers) and GPT (Generative Pretrained Transformer) have taken NLP to the next level, powering applications like chatbots, translation models, and AI-generated text.

This chapter explores:

- Understanding Sequential Data & Time Series – Why traditional models struggle with sequential data.
- RNNs, LSTMs, and GRUs – How deep learning handles sequential dependencies.
- Introduction to Transformers (BERT, GPT) – The state-of-the-art architecture for NLP.

Understanding Sequential Data & Time Series

13.1 What is Sequential Data?

Sequential data consists of data points arranged in a meaningful order where the position of an element influences its interpretation.

Examples of Sequential Data:
Text (NLP): Sentences where the order of words matters (e.g., "AI is powerful" vs. "Powerful AI is").
 Speech Recognition: Audio signals evolve over time.
Stock Market Prediction: Financial data where today's price depends on previous days.
 Weather Forecasting: Future temperatures depend on past climate conditions.
102

13.2 Challenges with Traditional Models

Traditional machine learning models, like decision trees or fully connected neural networks, treat all inputs independently, making them ineffective for sequential tasks.

Problem	Why Traditional Models Fail?
Word Order Matters	"The dog chased the cat" ≠ "The cat chased the dog"
Context Dependency	The meaning of a word depends on previous words ("bank" → financial vs. riverbank).
Long-Term Dependencies	Models struggle to retain information from earlier inputs.

To address these challenges, we use Recurrent Neural Networks (RNNs), Long Short-Term Memory (LSTMs), and Transformers.

RNNs, LSTMs, and GRUs

13.3 What is a Recurrent Neural Network (RNN)?

A Recurrent Neural Network (RNN) is a type of neural network designed to process sequential data by maintaining a hidden state that carries information from previous steps.

$$h_t = f(W_x X_t + W_h h_{t-1} + b)$$

Where:

- X_t: Input at time step t.
- h_t: Hidden state at time step t, which stores past information.
- h_{t-1}: Hidden state from the previous time step.
- W_x, W_h: Learnable weight matrices for input and hidden state connections.
- b: Bias term.
- f: Activation function (commonly **Tanh** or **ReLU**), adding non-linearity.

13.4 Implementing a Simple RNN in TensorFlow

python

CopyEdit

```python
import tensorflow as tf

from tensorflow.keras.models import Sequential

from tensorflow.keras.layers import SimpleRNN, Dense


# Define an RNN model

model = Sequential([

    SimpleRNN(50, activation='relu', input_shape=(10, 1)),   # 10
time steps, 1 feature per step

    Dense(1)  # Output layer for regression

])
```

```
# Compile the model

model.compile(optimizer='adam', loss='mse')


print(model.summary())
```

13.5 The Vanishing Gradient Problem

RNNs suffer from vanishing gradients, meaning that as sequences get longer, earlier information gradually fades, making it difficult for the model to learn long-term dependencies.

To solve this, LSTMs (Long Short-Term Memory networks) and GRUs (Gated Recurrent Units) introduce gates to regulate how much information is remembered or forgotten.

13.6 Long Short-Term Memory Networks (LSTMs)

LSTMs introduce three gates:

1. Forget Gate – Decides which past information to discard.
2. Input Gate – Determines what new information to store.
3. Output Gate – Selects what part of the memory to output.

ht=ot×tanh(ct)h_t = o_t \times tanh(c_t)ht=ot×tanh(ct)

where ctc_tct is the memory cell storing long-term dependencies.

Example: LSTM for Text Classification in TensorFlow

python

CopyEdit

```
from tensorflow.keras.layers import LSTM, Embedding
```

```
# Define LSTM model

model = Sequential([

    Embedding(input_dim=5000, output_dim=64),   # Word embedding
layer

    LSTM(100, return_sequences=False),   # LSTM layer

    Dense(1, activation='sigmoid')   # Output layer for binary
classification

])


model.compile(optimizer='adam', loss='binary_crossentropy',
metrics=['accuracy'])

print(model.summary())
```

LSTMs work well for long sequences but are computationally expensive.

13.7 Gated Recurrent Units (GRUs) – A Faster Alternative

GRUs simplify LSTMs by combining the forget and input gates into a single update gate.

$$h_t = z_t \times h_{t-1} + (1 - z_t) \times \tilde{h}_t$$

Example: GRU in TensorFlow

python

CopyEdit

```
from tensorflow.keras.layers import GRU


# Define GRU model

model = Sequential([

    Embedding(input_dim=5000, output_dim=64),

    GRU(100, return_sequences=False),  # GRU layer

    Dense(1, activation='sigmoid')

])


model.compile(optimizer='adam', loss='binary_crossentropy',
metrics=['accuracy'])
```

GRUs are faster and require fewer parameters than LSTMs.

Introduction to Transformers (BERT, GPT)

13.8 The Transformer Model: The Future of NLP

RNNs and LSTMs process data sequentially, making training slow. Transformers, introduced by Vaswani et al. (2017), revolutionized NLP by processing sequences in parallel, dramatically improving performance.

Key Innovation: The Self-Attention Mechanism

- Instead of processing words one at a time (like RNNs), transformers compute attention scores for all words in a sentence at once.
- This allows transformers to capture long-range dependencies efficiently.

13.9 BERT (Bidirectional Encoder Representations from Transformers)

BERT, developed by Google, is a bidirectional model trained on large text corpora.Understands word context based on surrounding words.
Used in search engines, chatbots, and question-answering systems.

Example: Using Pretrained BERT in Python

python

CopyEdit

```
from transformers import BertTokenizer,
TFBertForSequenceClassification


tokenizer = BertTokenizer.from_pretrained('bert-base-uncased')

model =
TFBertForSequenceClassification.from_pretrained('bert-base-uncas
ed')


inputs = tokenizer("Deep learning is powerful!",
return_tensors="tf")

outputs = model(**inputs)
```

13.10 GPT (Generative Pretrained Transformer) for Text Generation

GPT (OpenAI's Generative Pretrained Transformer) is a decoder-only transformer trained to generate human-like text.

Used in ChatGPT, AI writing tools, and language modeling.
Excels at generating coherent, context-aware responses.

Example: Using GPT for Text Generation

python

```
from transformers import GPT2Tokenizer, TFGPT2LMHeadModel

tokenizer = GPT2Tokenizer.from_pretrained("gpt2")
model = TFGPT2LMHeadModel.from_pretrained("gpt2")

input_text = "Artificial intelligence is"
input_ids = tokenizer.encode(input_text, return_tensors="tf")

output = model.generate(input_ids, max_length=50)
print(tokenizer.decode(output[0], skip_special_tokens=True))
```

GPT models generate human-like responses and are widely used in AI chatbots.

Key Takeaways from RNNs & Transformers for NLP

Technique	Best Use Case
RNNs	Short-term sequence tasks
LSTMs	Long-term dependencies (e.g., speech recognition)
GRUs	Faster alternative to LSTMs

BERT	NLP understanding (chatbots, search engines)
GPT	AI-generated text (writing, storytelling)

Deep learning has transformed NLP, enabling AI to understand, generate, and translate text like never before. The next chapter will explore deploying AI models and real-world applications.

Chapter 14

AI Model Deployment

Deploying an AI model is the final step in the machine learning pipeline, enabling models to be used in real-world applications such as web services, mobile applications, IoT devices, and cloud environments. AI deployment ensures that models serve predictions efficiently, securely, and at scale.

This chapter covers:

- Saving and Loading Models (Pickle, Joblib) – Storing trained models for later use.
- Deploying Models with Flask and FastAPI – Building APIs to serve AI predictions.
- Model Monitoring & Performance Tuning – Ensuring long-term efficiency and accuracy of deployed models.

Saving and Loading Models (Pickle, Joblib)

Once a model is trained, it needs to be saved and reused without retraining every time. Python provides Pickle and Joblib, two powerful libraries for serializing and deserializing AI models.

14.1 Saving Models with Pickle

Pickle is a built-in Python module that serializes (saves) objects into files and later loads them into memory.

Saving a Model Using Pickle

python

CopyEdit

```
import pickle

from sklearn.ensemble import RandomForestClassifier
```

```python
# Train a sample model

model = RandomForestClassifier(n_estimators=100)

X_train, y_train = [[1,2], [2,3], [3,4]], [0, 1, 1]

model.fit(X_train, y_train)


# Save the model

with open('model.pkl', 'wb') as f:

    pickle.dump(model, f)


print("Model saved successfully!")
```

Loading a Model Using Pickle

python

CopyEdit

```python
# Load the model

with open('model.pkl', 'rb') as f:

    loaded_model = pickle.load(f)


# Predict using the loaded model

X_test = [[2,3]]

print("Prediction:", loaded_model.predict(X_test))
```

14.2 Using Joblib for Large Models

Joblib is more efficient than Pickle for large datasets because it uses compressed binary storage.

Saving and Loading Models with Joblib

python

CopyEdit

```python
import joblib


# Save the model

joblib.dump(model, 'model.joblib')


# Load the model

loaded_model = joblib.load('model.joblib')


print("Model loaded successfully!")
```

When to Use Pickle? – For small models and quick experiments.
When to Use Joblib? – For large models and high-performance applications.

Deploying Models with Flask and FastAPI

Once an AI model is ready, it must be served to users via an API. The most common methods for deployment include Flask and FastAPI, which create web-based endpoints that allow users to interact with the model.

14.3 Deploying AI Models with Flask

Flask is a lightweight web framework that makes it easy to wrap an AI model into a REST API.

Step 1: Install Flask

bash

CopyEdit

```bash
pip install flask
```

Step 2: Create a Flask API for Model Serving

python

CopyEdit

```python
from flask import Flask, request, jsonify

import pickle

import numpy as np


# Load the model

with open('model.pkl', 'rb') as f:

    model = pickle.load(f)


app = Flask(__name__)


@app.route('/predict', methods=['POST'])

def predict():
```

```
data = request.get_json()

features = np.array(data['features']).reshape(1, -1)

prediction = model.predict(features).tolist()

return jsonify({'prediction': prediction})


if __name__ == '__main__':

    app.run(debug=True)
```

Step 3: Test the API with Postman or cURL

Send a POST request with JSON data:

json

CopyEdit

```
{

  "features": [2, 3]

}
```

Expected response:

json

CopyEdit

```
{

  "prediction": [1]

}
```

Flask is great for simple AI deployments but lacks high-speed performance.

14.4 Deploying AI Models with FastAPI

FastAPI is a modern alternative to Flask that supports asynchronous execution, making it faster and more scalable.

Step 1: Install FastAPI and Uvicorn

bash

CopyEdit

```
pip install fastapi uvicorn
```

Step 2: Create a FastAPI Model API

python

CopyEdit

```python
from fastapi import FastAPI

import joblib

import numpy as np


# Load the trained model
model = joblib.load('model.joblib')


app = FastAPI()


@app.post("/predict")
def predict(features: list):
    features_array = np.array(features).reshape(1, -1)
```

```
    prediction = model.predict(features_array).tolist()

    return {"prediction": prediction}


# Run the API server
if __name__ == "__main__":

    import uvicorn

    uvicorn.run(app, host="0.0.0.0", port=8000)
```

Step 3: Test the API

Send a POST request with JSON:

json

CopyEdit

```
{

  "features": [2, 3]

}
```


Expected response:

json

CopyEdit

```
{

  "prediction": [1]

}
```

FastAPI is faster and better for production use compared to Flask.

Model Monitoring & Performance Tuning

Once a model is deployed, it must be monitored and updated to maintain performance. Factors like data drift, model degradation, and user feedback require continuous evaluation.

14.5 Monitoring AI Models in Production

- Model Performance Metrics: Track accuracy, precision, recall, and F1-score over time.
- Data Drift Detection: Check if incoming data differs significantly from training data.
- Logging and Alerts: Set up logs to detect unusual model behavior.

Example: Logging Predictions

python

CopyEdit

```
import logging


logging.basicConfig(filename='model_logs.log',
level=logging.INFO)


def log_prediction(input_data, prediction):
    logging.info(f"Input: {input_data}, Prediction:
{prediction}")


log_prediction([2, 3], 1)
```

14.6 Automating Model Updates

As data changes over time, models may need retraining. An automated pipeline ensures the model stays up to date.

Example: Retraining Model Automatically

python

CopyEdit

```python
import schedule

import time


def retrain_model():

    print("Retraining model...")

    # (Code to load new data, retrain, and save model)


# Schedule retraining every week

schedule.every().week.do(retrain_model)


while True:

    schedule.run_pending()

    time.sleep(60)
```

Automating retraining helps maintain model accuracy over time.

Key Takeaways from AI Model Deployment

Step	Key Tools
Save & Load Models	Pickle (small models), Joblib (large models)
Deploy Model APIs	Flask (simple), FastAPI (high-performance)
Monitor Model in Production	Logging, data drift detection
Automate Model Updates	Scheduling retraining pipelines

Deploying an AI model allows it to serve real-world users, making predictions accessible via web applications, mobile devices, or cloud services. The next chapter will explore real-world AI applications in healthcare, finance, business, and more.

Chapter 15: Real-World AI Applications

Artificial Intelligence (AI) has transformed multiple industries, improving efficiency, accuracy, and automation in ways never seen before. AI models are now embedded in healthcare, finance, business, manufacturing, and entertainment, where they drive decision-making, automate processes, and enhance customer experiences.

However, as AI becomes more prevalent, it raises significant ethical concerns, including bias, data privacy, job displacement, and accountability. Understanding the potential and limitations of AI is crucial for ensuring its responsible and beneficial use.

This chapter explores:

- AI in Healthcare, Finance, and Business – Real-world use cases and impact.
- Ethical Considerations in AI – Bias, privacy, fairness, and regulations.

AI in Healthcare, Finance, and Business

15.1 AI in Healthcare

AI is revolutionizing healthcare by enabling faster diagnoses, personalized treatments, and predictive analytics. From medical imaging to robotic surgeries, AI-powered systems are reducing human errors and enhancing patient care.

AI Use Cases in Healthcare

Application	Description	Example AI Model
Medical Imaging	AI detects anomalies in X-rays, MRIs, CT scans	Deep Learning (CNNs)
Disease Diagnosis	AI predicts diseases based on symptoms and medical history	Decision Trees, Random Forest

Personalized Medicine	AI tailors drug recommendations based on genetic data	Reinforcement Learning
Robotic Surgery	AI assists in precision surgical operations	Computer Vision
Patient Monitoring	AI-powered wearable devices track health metrics	IoT + AI

Example: AI in Medical Imaging (Using CNNs)

python

CopyEdit

```python
from tensorflow.keras.models import load_model

import numpy as np

from tensorflow.keras.preprocessing import image


# Load pre-trained medical imaging model
model = load_model("medical_cnn_model.h5")


# Load and preprocess an X-ray image
img = image.load_img("xray_sample.jpg", target_size=(224, 224))

img_array = image.img_to_array(img) / 255.0

img_array = np.expand_dims(img_array, axis=0)
```

```python
# Predict if the image shows pneumonia or not

prediction = model.predict(img_array)

print("Prediction:", "Pneumonia Detected" if prediction > 0.5
else "No Pneumonia")
```

AI in Healthcare improves diagnostic accuracy, speeds up treatment, and enables remote monitoring.

15.2 AI in Finance

AI is reshaping the finance industry by improving fraud detection, risk assessment, trading, and customer service.

AI Use Cases in Finance

Application	Description	Example AI Model
Fraud Detection	Identifies suspicious transactions in real-time	Anomaly Detection
Credit Scoring	Predicts a borrower's likelihood to repay a loan	Logistic Regression, Random Forest
Algorithmic Trading	AI executes high-frequency stock trades	Reinforcement Learning

Customer Service	AI chatbots assist customers 24/7	NLP (Transformers)

Example: AI for Fraud Detection

python

CopyEdit

```python
from sklearn.ensemble import IsolationForest

import numpy as np


# Simulated transaction data

transactions = np.array([[500], [2000], [15000], [50], [70000]])
# Amounts in dollars


# Train an anomaly detection model

model = IsolationForest(contamination=0.1)

model.fit(transactions)


# Predict if a transaction is fraudulent (outlier)

prediction = model.predict([[70000]])  # Large transaction

print("Fraud Detected" if prediction == -1 else "Transaction
Normal")
```

 AI in Finance enhances fraud prevention, automates decision-making, and optimizes trading strategies.

15.3 AI in Business and Industry

Businesses use AI to streamline operations, enhance customer experiences, and improve productivity. AI is embedded in supply chains, HR, marketing, and cybersecurity.

AI Use Cases in Business

Application	Description	Example AI Model
Customer Support Chatbots	AI handles customer queries 24/7	NLP (GPT, BERT)
Supply Chain Optimization	Predicts inventory demand and logistics	Time-Series Forecasting
Marketing & Ad Targeting	AI personalizes advertisements based on user behavior	Recommendation Systems
Cybersecurity	AI detects security breaches and anomalies	Anomaly Detection

Example: AI Chatbot for Customer Service

python

CopyEdit

```
from transformers import pipeline
```

```
# Load a pre-trained chatbot model

chatbot = pipeline("text-generation",
model="microsoft/DialoGPT-medium")


# Simulating a customer query

response = chatbot("Hello, I need help with my
order.")[0]["generated_text"]

print("Chatbot Response:", response)
```

AI in Business automates tasks, improves customer interactions, and enhances decision-making.

Ethical Considerations in AI

As AI continues to evolve, ethical concerns must be addressed to ensure fairness, transparency, and accountability.

15.4 Bias in AI Models

AI models can inherit biases from their training data, leading to unfair outcomes.

Example of AI Bias:

- Hiring Algorithms rejecting candidates based on race or gender.
- Facial Recognition misidentifying individuals from certain ethnic backgrounds.

Solution: Use diverse training datasets, bias detection tools, and fairness-aware AI algorithms.

15.5 Data Privacy & Security

AI relies on vast amounts of data, raising concerns about user privacy and security.

Key Risks:

- Data Leaks – AI systems handling sensitive information (e.g., medical records) must prevent breaches.
- User Tracking – AI-driven personalization in social media and e-commerce can violate privacy.

 Solution: Implement data encryption, anonymization, and compliance with GDPR (General Data Protection Regulation) standards.

15.6 Job Displacement & Economic Impact

AI automation is replacing jobs in sectors like manufacturing, customer service, and retail, raising concerns about unemployment.

Examples of AI Automation:

- Self-Checkout Machines reducing the need for cashiers.
- AI-powered HR Systems automating resume screening and hiring.

Solution: Governments and industries must invest in AI-driven upskilling programs to help workers adapt.

15.7 Explainability & Accountability in AI

Many AI models, especially deep learning networks, operate as black boxes, making it difficult to explain why a model made a specific decision.

Example:

- A bank's AI denies a loan application without explaining why.

 Solution: Use Explainable AI (XAI) techniques like SHAP (SHapley Additive Explanations) to interpret model predictions.

Example: Using SHAP for AI Explainability

python

CopyEdit

```
import shap

import xgboost


# Train a simple AI model

X, y = [[1], [2], [3]], [0, 1, 1]

model = xgboost.XGBClassifier().fit(X, y)


# Explain model predictions

explainer = shap.Explainer(model)

shap_values = explainer(X)

shap.summary_plot(shap_values, X)
```

Key Takeaways from Real-World AI Applications

Industry	AI Impact
Healthcare	AI improves diagnostics, patient monitoring, and medical imaging.
Finance	AI enhances fraud detection, risk assessment, and algorithmic trading.

Business	AI automates customer service, marketing, and supply chain management.
Ethical AI	AI must be fair, transparent, and secure to avoid bias and harm.

AI is transforming industries, but it must be developed responsibly to maximize benefits while minimizing ethical risks.

With AI continuing to evolve, future advancements will include better explainability, regulation, and integration into everyday life, shaping how humans and machines interact.

www.ingramcontent.com/pod-product-compliance
Lightning Source LLC
LaVergne TN
LVHW051656050326
832903LV00032B/3854